The Perfect Fit

How to
Start an Image Consulting Business

Lynne Henderson Marks, AICI, CIP
Dominique Isbecque, AICI, CIP

Third Edition
November 2002

Illustrated by Deneb Toraño

Requests for permission to make copies of any part of this work should be mailed to:

Lynne Marks
London Image Institute
4279 Roswell Road, #102 PMB-318
Atlanta, GA 30342

"The Perfect Fit: How to Start an Image Consulting Business." ISBN 1-58939-290-6.

Published 2002 by Virtualbookworm.com Publishing Inc., P.O. Box 9949, College Station, TX, 77842, US. Copyright No. TX 5-488-742 © 2000, 2002 London Image Institute. All rights reserved. No part of this publication may be reproduced, stored in a retrieval system, or transmitted in any form or by any means, electronic, mechanical, recording or otherwise, without the prior written permission of the authors.

Manufactured in the United States of America.

ACKNOWLEDGMENTS

Each person who has crossed our paths has contributed to this book in some form or other. To each person we extend deeply felt gratitude. We have had many teachers along the was and not all have been in the classroom. Perhaps the most important gifts we have learned are the gifts to teach, empower others and create solutions. Our families, friends, students, clients, and colleagues have all been our teachers, giving us the opportunity to learn, teach, and continue to refine our skills. They have also been very patient and supportive of us during the glorious hours of this journey.

From the Association of Image Consultants International (AICI), we have so many colleagues from around the globe who over the years have shared their ideas, discoveries and challenges with us. People who come into contact with AICI members remark how unique it is to find a group of competitors who take more than a casual interest in everyone's success. The phrase "Together we grow" is taken to heart. When any consultant experiences a win, it is also another win for the profession. Our hope is that this book will shorten the path to success for image consultants, or at least shed light along the way.

To each of Dominique's interns, we cannot say "Thank you" enough for the hours and hours of work you have spent. You researched, proofread, made phone calls and kept the energy and momentum moving for the book while providing invaluable balance in Dominique's life. But most of all we thank you for your spirit of dedication and the commitment that you have to yourselves and your personal development. To Carol Davidson, Stephanie Winters, Nancy Altman, Sharon Kornstein, Linda Melloy, and MaryAnne Kokidis, we hope this energy is cyclic and will make your businesses soar.

Some people edit and change the meanings of words, and others read words, edit them and make them crystal clear. Lauren Solomon is one of those editors who brings crystal clarity to the English language, and we thank her for this. Thanks also to Diane Holleran for designing and formatting the first edition in record time. A very important part of the process were all the AICI professional members who filled out the surveys and the master assessment.

We would like to extend special thanks to Max Tabla, our desktop designer extraordinaire and quality control guru; Ruth Zanes, who generously contributed her coaching article; Bob Land, our final editor who added clarity and sparkle to the text; and Andover Franchising Inc., the authors of the WorkPerfect profile. Last but not least we would like to thank Deneb Toraño, whose illustrations provided delightful humor and wit to The Perfect Fit.

To all the future image consultants coming into this richly rewarding profession, we want to encourage you to each find your way. Always proceed fueled by your personal passion, commitment to excellence, and willingness to learn new talents. Keep your eyes and hearts open to the exciting possibilities available to all of us by working together. We wish you all great success!

Lynne Henderson Marks
Dominique Isbecque

Contents

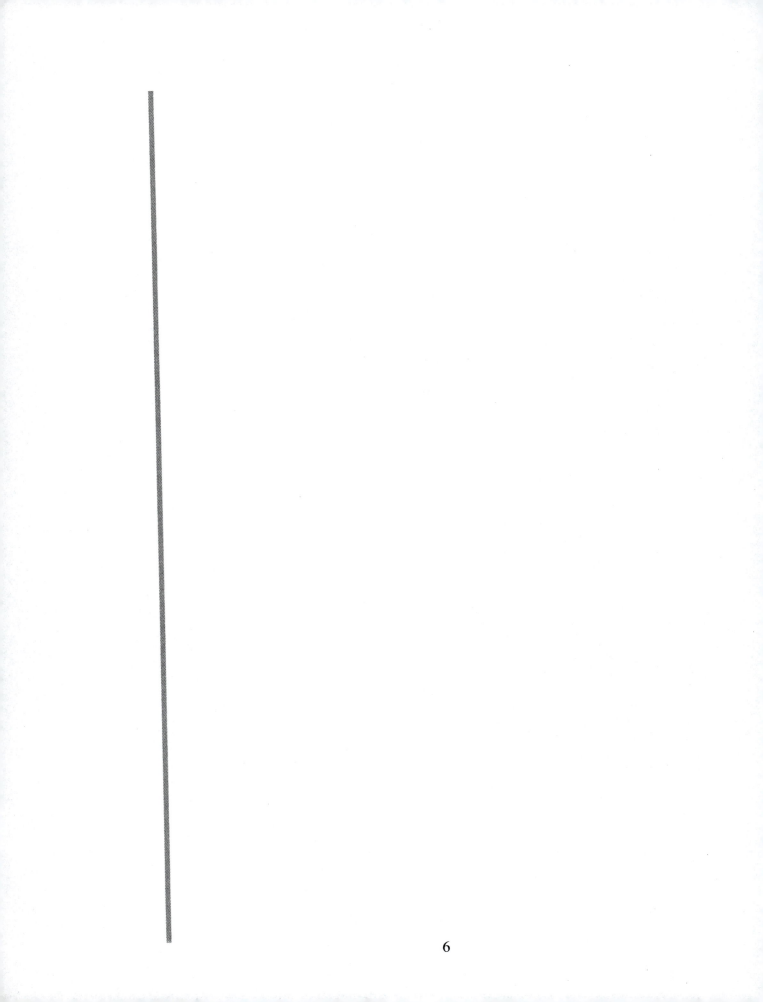

SECTION 1
What It's All About

INTRODUCTION

An image consultant is someone who specializes in visual appearance, verbal communication and nonverbal communication. He or she counsels both individual and corporate clients and addresses groups and organizations on appearance, behavior, communication skills and etiquette.

People come into image consulting through a myriad of ways, and none is better than the others. The main thing to realize when starting a career in this field is that image consulting is comprised of a variety of skills, talents and experiences. The more you accomplish and hone your skills, the better you can serve your clients.

Regardless of what your past work or personal life has been, this practical guide will show you which image consulting doors may be right for you. We have developed this book to answer many of the questions we hear every day and guide you through the choices available to you in the image consulting profession.

"The future belongs to those who believe in the beauty of their dreams."
—Eleanor Roosevelt

CHAPTER ONE

What Does an Image Consultant Do?

An image consultant can have a variety of specialties. There are style, color, and wardrobe consultants; media and public speaking trainers for verbal and nonverbal presentation skills; career coaches, teachers, authors, personal shoppers, cosmetic and skin care specialists, hair stylists, clothing and accessory designers, product developers, and etiquette experts.

Television personalities, politicians, and people in the public eye have always known the power of image. Now image enhancement is available to everyone. Clients enlist the aid of an image consultant to enhance their appearance and to improve their communication and social skills for many reasons. Many people in these fields report that they gained more self-confidence after an image makeover. Among other reasons, people go to an image consultant to look and feel better, increase their chances of promotion, find a partner or gain the competitive edge in an interview or at work. Politicians seek the assistance of image strategists to help them find the look and communication styles that appeal to voters. Television personalities are sometimes advised to soften or crisp up their image, change their hairstyles, and wear styles and colors more suitable for the camera.

Image consultants have a variety of skills, talents, and experiences. They know how to transform someone's image, and they also appreciate and love working with people. In most cases, their primary professional objective is to contribute to the success of others and help them maximize their potential.

The more you accomplish and hone your skills, the better you can serve your clients. This practical guide to starting an image consulting business will lead you through the first steps in developing your business. You will find out whether you are suited to the life of an entreprenuer and where your strengths lie, what further image skills you need, and how to build a viable, profitable business.

Where Do You Start If You Have No Experience?

As a curious observer to the field of image, you have discovered an aptitude and a talent for dressing your friends. You put yourself together with flair, and you like working with people. You are thinking of image consulting as a career. At this stage you may be wondering what training you should take or how you can increase your experience. Many avenues are open to you.

"Begin somewhere; you cannot build a reputation on what you intend to do."
—Liz Smith

The Association of Image Consultants International (AICI) has developed a core curriculum that outlines the skills you will need to serve your clients and to set up your business (see chapter 4). Image consulting demands not only skills pertinent to appearance, but also a deep appreciation of people themselves. The core curriculum reflects those qualities essential to becoming a successful image consultant and gives you an idea of the training you need to develop yourself further. The elective and advanced curricula outline other skills and experiences deemed necessary to build or expand a business and forge a well-established career.

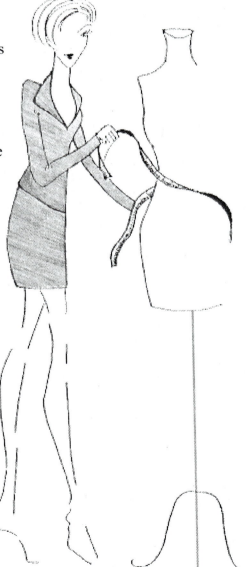

If you have no practical experience or training that corresponds to the core curriculum, and no idea if you will enjoy image consulting, you might seek local employment as a temporary measure. Working in a boutique or doing retail sales may help you decide whether or not you are suited to image as a career.

To gain entrepreneurial experience, you could also become a makeup representative; have your own color, jewelry, or clothing line; or work at an apparel store during the five or six week-long wholesale markets available each year.

If you know that you love to work with people on their image but lack some of the basic skills, then you could consider training. Some companies specialize in beginner's skills (see list of training companies). Some firms have the added advantage of offering product or computer backup services to help launch your company, enhance your services and add credibility and support to your name.

A few training companies and colleges take students with no experience. These institutions offer comprehensive long-term programs or correspondence courses and are built upon an organized curriculum, designed to take the student step-by-step through the basics of image consulting (see list of trainers). Internships are a wonderful way to learn what the job entails and to gain experience. You will be most fortunate if you find an internship that is both in your area of interest and in your geographic region. Large stores such as Macy's sometimes provide internship opportunities, as do some well-established image consultants.

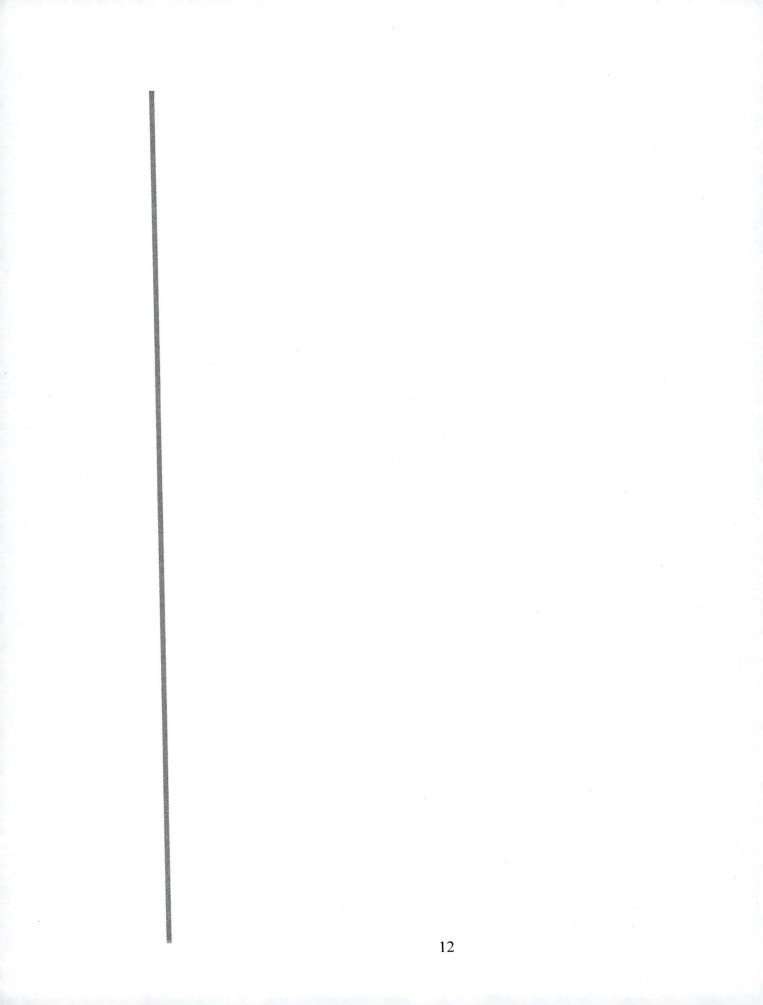

CHAPTER TWO

Are You the Perfect Fit?

What are the strengths and skills needed to equip yourself for a successful career in image consulting? We wanted to find out for ourselves what it took to be a successful image consultant, so we invited our professional colleagues at AICI to complete a survey. From their responses, a team of practitioners skilled in statistical analysis and career aptitude analysis were able to construct a profile. This information is now available to you in this book.

In this chapter, we invite you to take a candid look at your skills and aptitudes for the field of image. We have provided a customized survey that will allow you to evaluate yourself from an entrepreneurial standpoint. We have also added evaluations to gauge your experience, technical skills, natural talents, and business acumen. Armed with this self-knowledge, you will recognize how well your natural talents can be applied. You will also quickly realize what it takes to become successful in this career and how you can adapt, learn about, and modify your own skills and behaviors to make you the perfect fit for your chosen career.

"He who knows others is wise; he knows himself is enlightened."
—Lao-Tzu

How We Constructed the
Perfect Fit Image Consulting Profile

We surveyed the professional members of the Association of Image Consultants International (AICI), some of whom have specialty niche markets and others who are generalists. This group of consultants has gone through a rigorous application process developed by AICI and achieved professional status in the industry.

The consultants who took the survey run the gamut from independent personal shoppers to corporate communications image consultants. The assessment we used was "The WorkPerfect Survey" shown in this chapter, extrapolating the core behavioral competencies of successful image consultants and measuring against the job functions. There are no right or wrong answers to the survey questions. From our research, we found indications of the types of activities at which successful image consultants excel. In this assessment, core behavioral competencies include *personal qualities, skills, and aptitudes.* **Personal qualities** include behavioral tendencies, sensitivities, and natural human characteristics. **Skills** are learned and practiced abilities in image, business, teaching, and technology. **Aptitudes** include ability or learning tendencies to acquire certain skills.

With this raw data we were then able to construct a customized matrix for the successful image consultant. Not only will this information assist you, the new image consultant, to focus on the competencies to become successful, but also it will show you where you may face challenges.

The assessment focuses on nine job functions that are often critical aspects of a successful business laid over the primary job functions of the image consultant. These job functions are:

- Entrepreneur
- Manager
- Administrator
- Sales
- Training
- Production or implementation of the job
- Customer service
- Counselor
- Technician

If you take the survey for yourself, you will receive a comprehensive evaluation of your profile. You will have a very good idea of the areas in which you are a natural fit and born to the job. You will also have a better understanding of how your strengths and limitations will affect your potential to succeed and what areas you will need to develop.

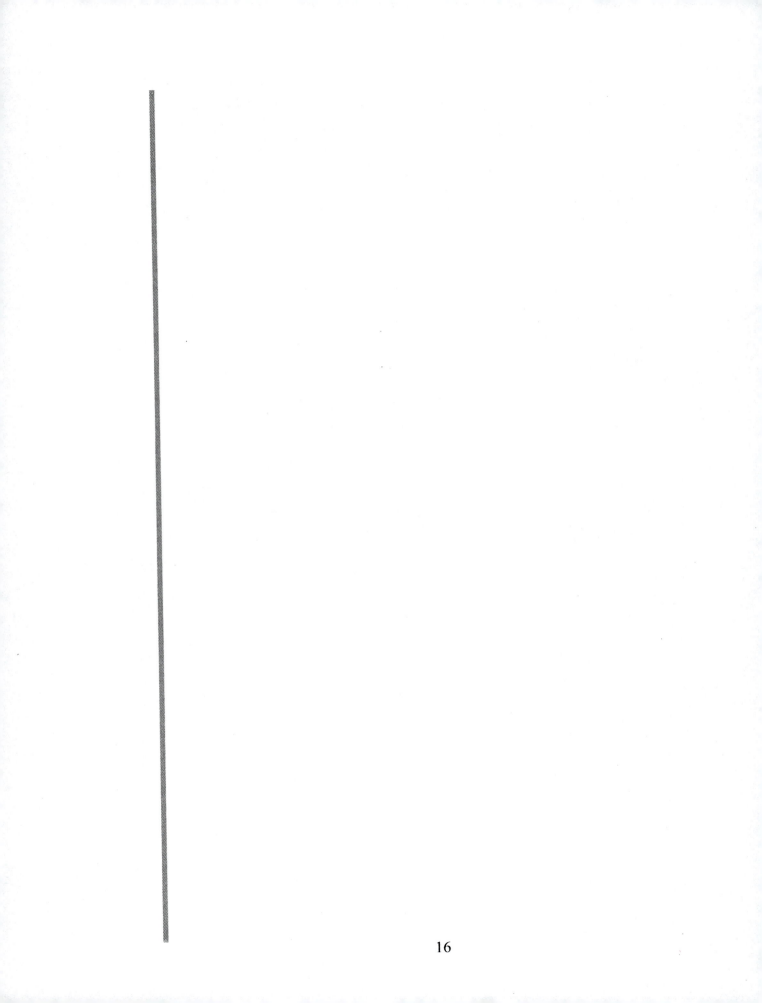

The Image Consultant WorkPerfect Survey

(Please fill in the details, answer all the questions and email to:
Lynnemarks@aol.com or fax the survey back to us at 404-303-8818)

Please provide the following information:

Please print or type:

Mr.

Ms. _____

Company _____

Mailing Address _____

City, State, Zip _____

Telephone _____ Ext. _____

Fax _____

E-mail Address _____

Payment Information:

o Check/Money Order enclosed payable to: **London Image Institute**
   Mail to: **4279 Roswell Road, #102-PMB318, Atlanta, GA 30342**

Charge to: o MasterCard   Card number _____

             o Visa   Expiration date _____

                                Signature _____

When you start any business you should determine which of your innate behavioral traits you should focus on to help you achieve your full potential. You are a "natural fit" in some job functions, but you'll have to "stretch" to be a star performer in other positions. Results of The WorkPerfect Survey will help you better understand your traits and guide you toward a business that capitalizes on your strengths.

Read each statement carefully. Select the response that most closely matches your feelings, attitudes, or actions. There are no right answers, and your first impulse is usually the most accurate. Work quickly without stopping to analyze each response. For the best results, limit your "Sometimes" responses to 10. Have fun and be sure to complete all 48 questions. Circle or underline the response you select. This exercise will take about fifteen minutes. Again, we suggest that you limit your "Sometimes" responses to a total of 10.

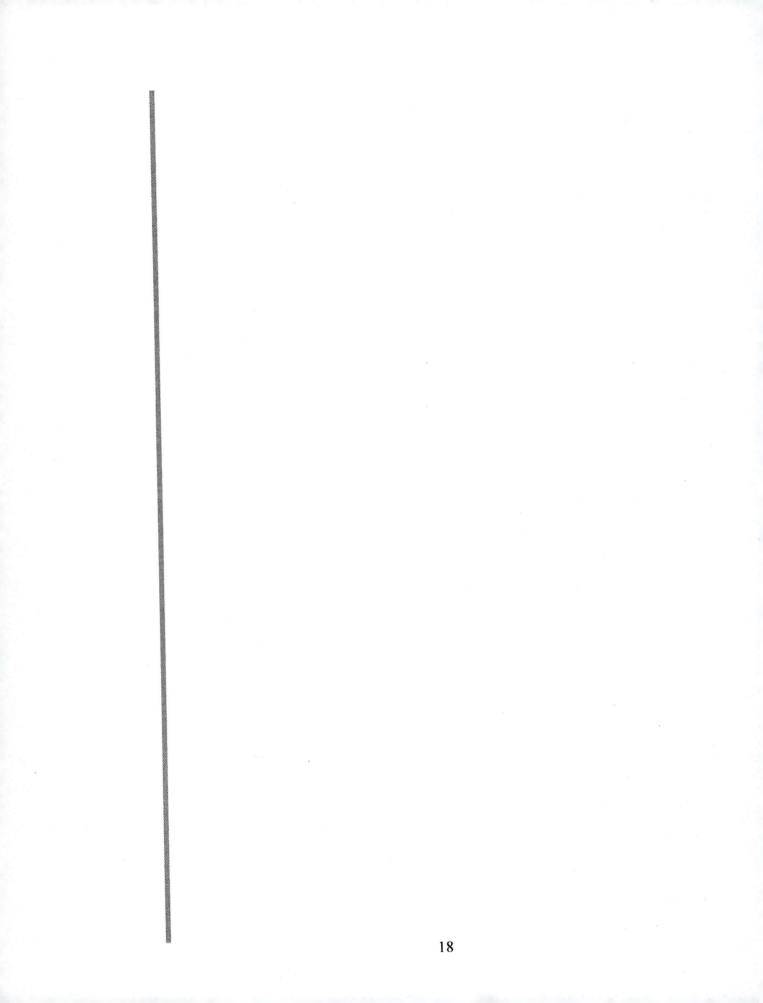

The Image Consultant Perfect Fit Survey

1.	I'd rather stay home than go out with friends.	Yes	No	Sometimes
2.	I read the directions before putting something together.	Yes	No	Sometimes
3.	I allow people to cut ahead of me in line.	Yes	No	Sometimes
4.	I prefer to serve on committees.	Yes	No	Sometimes
5.	The best vacations are planned out in advance.	Yes	No	Sometimes
6.	Trusting others is difficult.	Yes	No	Sometimes
7.	I tend to keep quiet when out with people I do not know well.	Yes	No	Sometimes
8.	I feel that strict guidelines make for better decisions.	Yes	No	Sometimes
9.	People say I don't rock the boat.	Yes	No	Sometimes
10.	After a job well done, everyone should get the same rewards.	Yes	No	Sometimes
11.	People say I am a perfectionist.	Yes	No	Sometimes
12.	I am described as carefree.	Yes	No	Sometimes
13.	I am at ease entering a room where most people are strangers.	Yes	No	Sometimes
14.	All things equal, I'll choose to go where I've never been before.	Yes	No	Sometimes
15.	People say I am a person who must have his own way.	Yes	No	Sometimes
16.	When things go wrong, people should share the blame.	Yes	No	Sometimes
17.	I enjoy taking care of details.	Yes	No	Sometimes
18.	I find myself tense under pressure.	Yes	No	Sometimes
19.	I like to take risks.	Yes	No	Sometimes
20.	There is a right way to do things.	Yes	No	Sometimes
21.	I am comfortable making decisions for others.	Yes	No	Sometimes
22.	Keeping score makes games more fun.	Yes	No	Sometimes
23.	I arrive early for meetings.	Yes	No	Sometimes
24.	I question other people's motives.	Yes	No	Sometimes
25.	I like to tell jokes.	Yes	No	Sometimes
26.	I like to take shortcuts in my work.	Yes	No	Sometimes
27.	I make decisions slowly.	Yes	No	Sometimes
28.	I enjoy being singled out from the group.	Yes	No	Sometimes
29.	I am uncomfortable working without a plan.	Yes	No	Sometimes
30.	Things always work out for the best.	Yes	No	Sometimes
31.	I like to be the life of the party.	Yes	No	Sometimes
32.	People say I am predictable.	Yes	No	Sometimes
33.	I am content to let things happen.	Yes	No	Sometimes
34.	Group decisions produce the best results.	Yes	No	Sometimes
35.	I like it when friends drop by unexpectedly.	Yes	No	Sometimes
36.	It takes time for me to recover from a disappointing setback.	Yes	No	Sometimes
37.	Listening is more fun for me than talking.	Yes	No	Sometimes
38.	Policies fail because there are exceptions to every rule.	Yes	No	Sometimes
39.	I am at my best supporting a good leader.	Yes	No	Sometimes
40.	It's important to listen to everyone's viewpoint before deciding.	Yes	No	Sometimes
41.	I feel that it is difficult to be on time.	Yes	No	Sometimes
42.	One look tells you how I feel.	Yes	No	Sometimes
43.	I prefer solitary activities.	Yes	No	Sometimes
44.	I like an established routine.	Yes	No	Sometimes
45.	I prefer to ask for forgiveness rather than ask for permission.	Yes	No	Sometimes
46.	It is important for me to win even if the team loses.	Yes	No	Sometimes
47.	I cannot get things done with a cluttered desk.	Yes	No	Sometimes
48.	I worry that I am not doing enough.	Yes	No	Sometimes

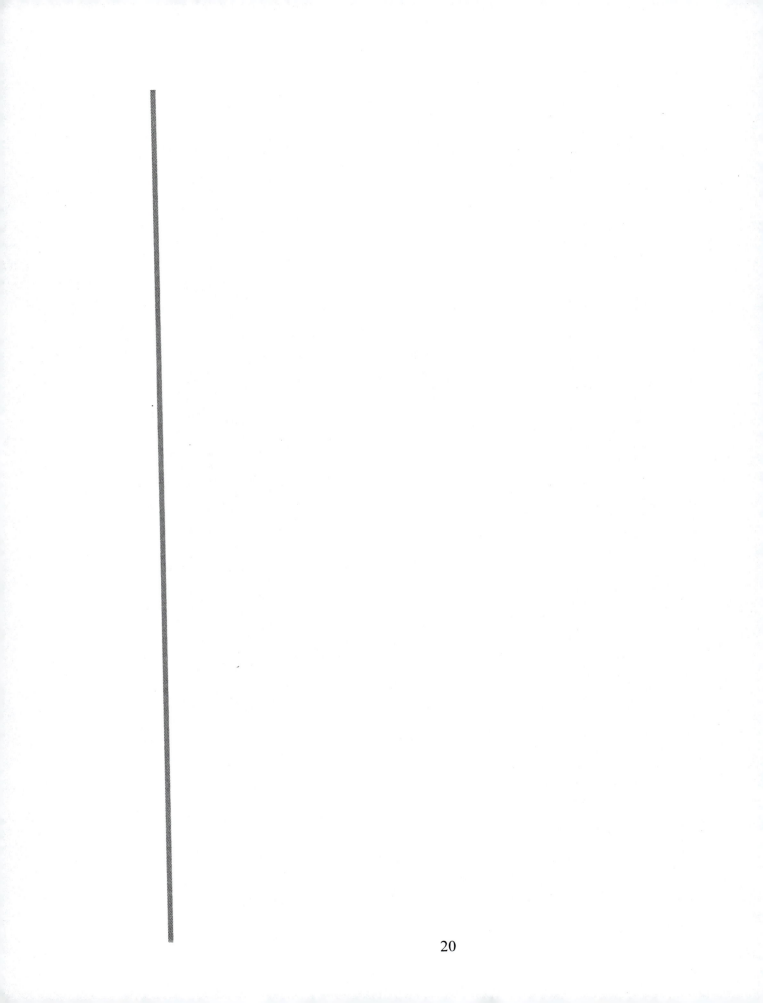

What We Learned About the Perfect Fit Image Consultant

Entrepreneurial image consultants tend to be extroverts. They communicate enthusiasm about their business and have the natural ability to attract people who will become their clients. They enjoy the chance to network, which is critical to developing most small businesses. Meeting new people and establishing relationships is natural to them and useful in building a customer base. They are also comfortable with the risk and challenges involved in being an entrepreneur. They have a dislike for repetitive tasks, solitude, and being ignored in a group. One of their main traits is a strong need for other people, and they depend on the support, encouragement, and social approval of others. They are challenged by the solitude of the start-up phase of a new business and need to find the right balance between socializing for recreation and socializing to avoid loneliness. However, extroverts need to find the right balance between socializing for recreation and socializing to avoid loneliness. In client interactions, they must remember to listen to clients' ideas and give them opportunities to participate in discussions. Successful image consultants are good at interacting with audiences and enjoy speaking to groups. They are gregarious, outgoing, and communicative.

"Accomplishment will prove to be a journey, not a destination."
—Dwight D. Eisenhower

Successful image consultants have a moderate need for structure and rules in their lives, yet are able to function without rigid guidelines. They can also manage changing environments without experiencing stress. In situations where they are exposed to extreme regulation with rigid policies—or constantly changing circumstances with no policies at all—they typically feel extremely challenged. They enjoy the seasonal changes in fashion and the variety of styles, colors, and image tools available to them. Image consultants have the ability to understand and identify with a wide range of clients and peers, and work with them effectively. They are outstanding in the area of service, since their clients appreciate both the dependability and the flexibility they provide to meet their needs.

Image consultants need to be balanced between assertiveness and support for their clients. They must be able to deal with a moderate level of confrontation. Extreme confrontation for extended periods is difficult for them, and could have an adverse effect on their work. They will take charge only when the situation demands it.

They will express their opinions directly, yet they recognize how their message will be received by others. Image consultants can modify their message depending on the personality they are dealing with, thus avoiding unnecessary confrontation. Since an image consultant's main role is to offer critiques on what is considered by most people a personal subject, they are not afraid to critique openly and are adept at critiquing in a manner that does not cause conflict or offense.

The successful image consultant is at his or her best as a team player. Team-oriented people are cooperative, noncompetitive, and friendship-oriented. Image consultants must seek win-win solutions for their clients in a non-threatening environment. Team-oriented consultants judge their success by how well they have "carried their own weight" in helping a client or a group achieve its goals. They are valued for their willingness to help others. They view cooperation as the best approach, rather than forcing an opinion on a client, and they enjoy seeing others succeed and grow.

The most successful image consultants tend to be organized, meaning that image consultants need a controlled, carefully planned, orderly environment. Organized consultants analyze all the details to ensure that they will meet deadlines and forestall mistakes. They are punctual, and they thrive in an environment that allows for follow-through, scheduling, and planning. They are involved with detail and enjoy detail-oriented aspects of the image consulting job such as coordinating outfits, choosing the right accessories, and matching colors. They are thorough and precise, and pick up on small but critical elements of a project or situation.

The successful image consultant is balanced between empathy and calm in the face of crisis. They are typically cool-headed and unflappable, yet still sensitive to the situation and the client's needs. In times of high emotion, they must know the signals of a true crisis and be ready to act. They react to the stress of others and show empathy without becoming emotionally involved in the situation. Clients respond well to consultants who seem to have the situation under control, yet also demonstrate a deep understanding of their needs. These traits of an image consultant are comforting for their clients. Image consultants do not fall apart at the first sign of failure, rejection, or disappointment; rather, they take these results in stride. They may feel rejected if a seminar or a consultation does not go as planned, yet they do not internalize criticism and failure, nor do they let these occurrences stand in the way of growth and development. The greatest strength of an image consultant is the outward appearance of relaxation, combined with the ability to both read emotional signs from clients, trainees, and coworkers and act on these signs with propriety and ease.

Profiled by Andover Consulting
July, 2000

Now You Can Evaluate Your Technical, Business, and Image Skills

As you reflect upon the following lists, rate yourself on a scale of one to five. **Be honest**. A **five** rating represents the highest level of competence or experience, and a **zero** represents no ability or experience. Your answers should reflect your level of awareness, experience, and comfort zone in each of the categories. Given the work of image consultants, honesty about your own strengths and limitations is paramount. You may be highly skilled in some areas and have less experience in others. The inventory results will help you prioritize your needs and plan your next steps. The results will also give you a blueprint of your current abilities and core competencies. Most of these traits can be developed. If you scored lower in certain areas, you may simply be best suited to a particular niche, or in need of training to round out your skills.

Please circle the number that most closely represents your level.

Image Consulting Skills

This group includes many of the core skills used daily in a professional image consulting practice. Your answers should reflect your ability and/or experience in utilizing these skills. **Zero** is no experience or ability, **Medium** is some experience or ability, and **High** is *Yes, I've done it for years and I know what I'm doing.* The way to determine whether your skills are High or Medium is as follows: If you can teach the abilities and skills and explain the principles behind them, you merit a High ranking. A Medium ranking indicates that you can perform the skills but cannot necessarily teach them to others.

	None	Low	Med	High
I am able to diagnose personal skin tone colors.	0	(1)	3	5
I am able to color coordinate wardrobes.	0	1	(3)	5
I know how to analyze figure types.	0	(1)	3	5
I understand balance and proporation.	0	(1)	3	5
I have knowledge of fabrics and textiles.	0	1	(3)	5
I have knowledge of clothing care.	0	1	(3)	5
I have fashion resources.	(0)	1	3	5
I know about fashion style/personality.	0	(1)	3	5
I have accessorizing skills.	0	(1)	3	5
I understand and appreciate beauty and aesthetics.	0	1	(3)	5
I know basic design principles and principles of harmony.	(0)	1	3	5
I understand garment construction and alterations.	0	1	3	(5)
I understand wardrobe planning.	0	1	(3)	5
I have selection and coordination strategies.	0	(1)	3	5
I have knowledge of fashion trends.	0	(1)	3	5
I understand strategic dressing.	0	(1)	3	5
I understand lifestyle planning.	0	1	(3)	5
I understand makeup application.	0	(1)	3	5
I know hairstyles and face shapes.	0	(1)	3	5
I understand skin care, hygiene, and grooming.	0	1	(3)	5
I work with color psychology.	(0)	1	3	5
I have some external methods to access my clients.	0	1	3	(5)
I transmit ideas and information clearly.	0	1	(3)	5
I am aware of regional dressing codes & image expectations.	(0)	1	3	5
I have a wardrobe planning methodology.	0	(1)	3	5
I can speak to groups.	0	(1)	3	5
I understand budgets and cost factors.	0	1	(3)	5
I address etiquette & business protocol.	0	1	(3)	5
I am skilled at non verbal communication (body language).	0	(1)	3	5
I can facilitate and/or teach image.	0	(1)	3	5
I utilize psychology of image.	(0)	1	3	5
I conduct closet/wardrobe audits.	(0)	1	3	5
I take people shopping.	0	1	(3)	5
Totals				

Business Skills
(management, sales & marketing, etc.)

This skill set enables a consultant to develop a viable, for-profit business. Identify your experience and level of mastery by ranking each of the following business skills and practices. These rankings should reflect your actual experience, *not* your comfort zone when *learning* the skill or practice.

	None	Low	Med	High
Accounting / Bookkeeping	0	1	(3)	5
Advertising	(0)	1	3	5
Business planning	0	(1)	3	5
Business writing	0	1	(3)	5
Cash flow management	0	(1)	3	5
Customer service	0	1	3	(5)
Goal setting	0	1	(3)	5
Management	0	1	3	(5)
Marketing	(0)	1	3	5
Negotiations	0	1	(3)	5
Networking	0	1	(3)	5
Organizing	0	1	(3)	5
Organizational development	0	1	3	5
Promotions	0	1	3	5
Public relations	0	1	3	5
Public speaking	0	1	3	5
Sales	0	1	3	5
Self-promotion	0	1	3	5
Special event development	0	1	3	5
Telephone sales	0	1	3	5
Time management	0	1	3	(5)
Vision and mission	0	1	3	5
Totals				

Technological Skills
(electronics, computer, etc.)

These skills are especially useful in a one-person operation. If you currently have or plan to have a staff, you may not need to have all of the following skills.

	None	Beginner	Intermed.	Advanced
Accounting software application	0	1	(3)	5
Computer assisted design	(0)	1	3	5
Computer imaging applications	(0)	1	3	5
Database operation	0	1	3	(5)
Desktop publishing	0	1	3	(5)
Digital image creation	(0)	1	3	5
Digital image transmission	(0)	1	3	5
E-commerce	0	1	(3)	5
E-mail	0	1	3	(5)
Internet research	0	1	3	(5)
Internet sales	(0)	1	3	5
Keyboard skills	0	1	3	(5)
Overhead projector operation	0	1	3	(5)
Slide projector operation	0	1	3	(5)
Technological presentations	0	1	3	(5)
Telephone sales	(0)	1	3	5
Use of slides & overheads	0	1	3	(5)
Video camera operation	0	1	3	(5)
Video player operation	0	1	3	(5)
Word processing	0	1	3	(5)
Website creation/design	0	1	(3)	5
Website maintenance	0	(1)	3	5
Totals				

Inventory of Technology, Business Tools, and Resources (equipment, financial, marketing)

This list identifies what technology, contacts, resources, and tools you have available. These needs will ultimately vary depending upon your business goals, client expectations, and your creativity and resourcefulness. You do not have to possess all of the items on this list. Technology and tools simply enable you to save time and perform certain services more easily. When you reach the section of this book dealing with the creation of your business, your particular needs will become apparent.

If you already have anything on this list, check off the **Own** column. If you have use of the item available to you, check off the **Borrow or share** column. Review this list and identify what you have available to you and/or plan to buy.

	Do not have	Borrow or share	Own
Assessment tools	(0)	3	5
Biography	0	(3)	5
Brochure	0	(3)	5
Business cards	0	3	(5)
CD-ROM capability	0	3	(5)
Cell phone	0	3	(5)
Consulting tools (for color, image)	(0)	3	5
Contacts and/or mailing lists	(0)	3	5
Designated business telephone	0	(3)	5
Designated office (home or office)	0	3	(5)
Digital camera	0	3	(5)
E-mail & internet access	0	3	(5)
Fax machine	0	3	(5)
Financial resources- seed money	0	3	(5)
Letterhead	0	3	(5)
Memberships & subscriptions	(0)	3	5
PC or Laptop	0	3	(5)
Printer	0	3	(5)
Professional wardrobe	0	3	(5)
Scanner	0	3	(5)
Software-Accounting	0	3	(5)
Word processing	0	3	(5)
Desktop publishing	0	3	(5)
Voice mail/answering service	0	3	(5)
Web-site	0	3	(5)
Workbook/materials	0	3	(5)
Totals			

Past Experience

Reflect on things you have done in your life and rate them into the following levels of experience. Remember that many non-paid activities bring excellent experience and leadership development.

	None	Some	A lot
Budget planning (household, business, volunteer)	0	3	(5)
Counseling/coaching (professional, family, camp, school, sports)	0	3	(5)
Event planning (vacations, Boy Scouts, community projects, family reunion)	0	3	(5)
Fashion, beauty*	(0)	3	5
Leadership (Girl/Boy Scouts, team captain)	0	3	(5)
Management of finances (household, business, Junior League)	0	3	(5)
Organizational experience (board participation)	(0)	3	5
Other project management (fundraising, managing a local political campaign)	0	3	(5)
A personal passion for this profession	0	3	(5)
Public speaking (social, PTA, volunteer)	(0)	3	5
Sales (retail, telemarketing)	0	(3)	5
Other	0	3	5
Totals			

* (fragrance & fashion modeling, cosmetic sales, skin care makeup consultant)

Your Personal Assessment Evaluation

Now that you have completed the personal assessment, let us see where you are in each of the sections. Place your totals below, then circle your range according to the **Low, Medium, High** scale.

	Your Scores	Low	Medium	High
Image consulting skills	57	0-50	51-100	101-170
Business skills		0-40	41-85	86-110
Technological skills	70	1-40	41-75	76-110
Inventory of tools and resources	104	0-40	41-95	96-130
Past experience	34	0-20	21-45	46-65

Where Do You Go from Here?

If you scored **High** in all categories, congratulations! You are ready to start your professional practice as an image consultant! You just need to choose your focus and determine your course of action.

If you scored in the **Medium** or **Low** ranges, then we suggest that you look at the particular areas that need strengthening and take courses or hire coaches to give you reinforcement in those areas.

In this guidebook, you will work on the steps to design and create your professional practice. As a new consultant, you will learn the actual essential skills and tools that you need to start, rather than skills and tools that may be useful but are not urgent. For example, a consultant who chooses to work in the corporate arena needs many more tools, skills, and perhaps experience to be successful, simply because the corporate world expects its consultants to operate at the highest levels. An image consultant must be as competent and experienced as any other consultant an organization would retain on its vendor list.

If you scored **Low** in any of the areas *and* your passion level is also low, we suggest that you reconsider your career choice. As an entrepreneur, being successful is difficult without both a high level of passion and strong technical skills. From our experience and observation of newcomers to the industry, we have seen many people who have begun a practice and then closed it down because they had insufficient training, lack of focus, and little entrepreneurial resilience or perseverance. A high level of passion acts as an essential fuel to motivate and catalyze you. Your passion helps mobilize all your resources to achieve personal success. Passion is also often the first reason clients hire you and people continue to support you.

"I realized early on that success was tied to not giving up. Most people in this business gave up and went on to other things. If you simply didn't give up, you would outlast the people who came in on the bus with you."
—Harrison Ford

CHAPTER THREE

What Career Opportunities Are Available?

What opportunities are there for careers in image consulting?

What are the different categories of image consulting?

What products and services can the image consultant sell?

What challenges can I expect?

Image consultants fall roughly into three primary categories:

1. Entrepreneurs who serve individual clients
2. Entrepreneurs who serve organizations
3. Permanent employees in an organization

Each category has its own set of services, marketing strategies, sales cycles, success expectations, risks and benefits, time commitments, client expectations, and required skill sets. Many consultants start out as one type, find they have an aptitude for another, and expand their services to include it. Some consultants offer all types of image consulting services from the beginning of their careers.

Image Consultants Who Serve Individual Clients

Image consultants who serve individual clients can be specialists or generalists. A generalist should be able to offer services such as color analysis, body type analysis, wardrobe, clothing and personal style analysis, closet assessments, personal shopping, makeup application, and accessory selection. A specialist may also be able to offer all these services, but in addition, he or she provides a specialized approach or service that may go beyond purely external image consulting. For example, image consultants to the individual market may also address a client's communication skills such as nonverbal and verbal communication, or social skills such as etiquette and protocol. Image consultants may be called upon to coach in life transition situations, such as changes in career and social or marital status. Specialties you may come across are Fashion Feng Shui experts, bridal consultants, etiquette consultants, and executive, career, or life coaches.

Image consultants also find that their skills are useful in paramedical situations, such as helping a client during cancer therapy or other convalescent periods. Not only are image consultants often a resource for other types of consultants, but image professionals frequently recommend other types of services to complement their own. For example, they may encourage their clients to work with fitness or diet experts, holistic mind/body practitioners, cosmetic dentists, cosmetic surgeons, or paramedical beauty and skin care consultants. Some image consultants may represent and sell products such as cosmetics, skin care, health and nutrition products, clothing, and accessories, while others will choose only to provide services. Selling products offers another stream of revenue to the consultant and often provides a lucrative profit center. For more information regarding companies offering products marketed through direct sales, see the appendix.

Fee Structure for Individual Consultants

The professional consultant to individuals may charge an hourly rate and/or offer packages and subscription services, and is paid upon delivery of services. Pre-shopping or research time is usually part of this service and can be billed to the client or built into the service fees.

Personal Shopping

A private personal shopper makes recommendations to the client and then fulfills his or her needs on a seasonal or ongoing basis. The shopper could also be commissioned by the client to buy gifts and organize closets. He may also be retained on a regular basis to serve as a valet, to transport and ship items, or to organize a client's image life.

Shoppers are asked to obtain items from an amazingly diverse list. For example, image consultants who are working as personal shoppers may shop for outfits for interviews, dates, weight loss or gain, maternity wear, wedding parties, physical challenges, resort and business travel, graduations, debutante balls, beauty pageants, media events and tours, evening wear, theme wear, and swim wear. Shoppers may also be commissioned to buy eyewear and gifts of clothing for holidays and special occasions.

Shopping for a client takes many different forms. You can go to the store alone, pull clothes, and meet the client later. The client can also accompany you to the store. Alternatively, you can bring the selections to the client's home at a designated time. You may also shop for clothes using a variety of resources. The first and most common resource is the retail market, such as large stores and boutiques. Second, wholesale vendors may be available in the apparel market of some cities, and you can visit their showrooms to see if they are selling off their samples at the end of the seasonal market. You may even come to know a manufacturer's representative and bring clients to buy samples at the end of the season. Third, many lines of clothing and other products are available from independent representatives—lines such as Doncaster, Juliana Collezione, Westbrook, Carlisle, French Rags, and Weekenders, as well as many men's custom-tailored lines. These sources for clothing are designed for people who have little time to shop, yet are interested in a quality look. As the consultant, you typically receive a sample line of clothes four or five times a year and set them up in a room of your house or a studio. You invite friends, neighbors, and clients to view and order from these sample garments and other fabric swatches in a comfortable, non-threatening environment.

Being a personal shopper has a few pitfalls. You might be brilliant and the envy of all your friends when it comes to putting yourself together, but trying to dress other people is a different matter altogether. You are not only dealing with appearance but also your client's personality and psychology. Fashion theory and the practical implications of working with a client are two separate issues! Matching the current styles to your clients' needs and body proportions is much harder than you may think. Clothes might not always be available in his or her size, color, fabric, or figure preference. The secret here is to gain practical experience, train your eye, and learn as much as possible about fit, fabric, and style personality. On the other hand, if you have prepared sufficiently for your client's needs and she or he still does not buy the clothes, you may also need to learn the gentle art of persuasion to help you "sell" the clothes to the client.

Closet Analysis (a.k.a. Closet Audit, Closet Inventory)

An image consultant is frequently asked to look into someone's closet and clear out the clothes that no longer suit a client's needs. In a closet analysis/audit/inventory, the consultant goes through the entire wardrobe, weeding out old, inappropriate clothes; creating new outfits with existing clothes; suggesting alterations and updates; and generally organizing the client's closet. People tend to keep clothes for emotional reasons, and a consultant can help a client enormously just by lending an impartial eye. Without any emotional attachment, the consultant can clear out undesirable garments and suggest improvements in style, color, fabric, and quality. She may even take the discarded clothes with her and donate them to charity.

One of the main challenges of doing a closet analysis is estimating the amount of time needed to do the job; image consultants often underestimate the time the task will take. A wise precaution is to give the client a range of time rather than an absolute. By finishing early you look more professional than if you run too long. Have a well-thought-out procedure for attacking a closet and explain your plan before starting the session, just in case the client really wants to do the job herself and take over!

Makeup Application and Sales

If you have an artistic talent, you will love to teach or sell makeup. Seeing a face enhanced with even a little makeup can be most rewarding. What's more, the client can quickly see herself in a new light and may be more open to further changes.

Makeup artists can choose from a variety of direct lines. You can buy a line from an established makeup company such as Mary Kay or BeautiControl, or you may choose to buy wholesale from the factory and put your own label on the merchandise. Many cosmetics lines also have excellent skincare products and other useful supplies and sales materials. You can also produce your own makeup line.

One of the major pitfalls in makeup application is the inability to consider the client's preferences and insensitivity to her personal taste in makeup. Wearing makeup may come naturally to us as image consultants, but to many people cosmetics feel like an unnatural mask. Whenever you are suggesting changes to your clients, a good policy is to test the amount of change you can actually make at one time, compared to the amount of change you think your client can handle. Again, these issues are more psychological than technical.

Color Analysis

Many consultants love to work with color, and clients are drawn to our services because of it. Color analysis is the craze that was introduced in 1980 with the publication of Carole Jackson's book, *Color Me Beautiful.* Clients may not be familiar with image consulting but will be open to having their "colors done" because they have read about it or have friends who have done it. For many clients, personal colors form the foundation of clothing and makeup decisions. Color can also form part of a strategic communication plan to help a client project particular messages. For example, a person interviewing for a highly aggressive sales position can wear colors that project assertiveness, whereas a counselor or therapist may choose colors that help others feel comfortable and nurtured.

Color analysis is part art, part science. Consultants use a methodology or systematic approach to color analysis, depending upon their objectives or purpose. Diagnostic tools, training, and color reference charts can all be part of servicing the client. A typical detailed color analysis might include draping the client: the consultant, by draping colored fabrics on the individual, carefully diagnoses the best colors for the client. The client often receives a reference booklet or fan of either silkscreened or fabric color swatches. The color reference chart is used in clothing selection, planning, and coordination. However, if the consultant's primary objective is to sell the client clothes or to perform a closet or shopping consultation, then the color analysis may be brief. The consultant might not necessarily drape the client, but instead examine her skin, hair, and eye tone, conducting the analysis from that information. In these cases, the consultant only needs basic color information in order to select and sell makeup or clothing.

In a customized color analysis session, on the other hand, the consultant will select from an inventory of hundreds of shades, tones, and hues, or may even hand-paint the client's palette. This session leads the client through a process of self-discovery; by the end, she will know in detail which colors are best suited to her natural coloring. She will also learn about the psychology of color and which colors are most appropriate to wear for different events, seasons, and ages in her life. Clients love learning about themselves through color.

The challenge of color analysis is first to select an approach that meets your business and aesthetic objectives. Many colorists train in more than one system because they are not certain of which one they will eventually use more frequently. Color can also be a very seductive medium. The more we learn about color, the more we are intrigued by it.

Tools for color analysis can be expensive, ranging in cost from $65 for basic indicator drapes to thousands of dollars for a custom color swatch inventory. Training hours also run the gamut. Training in color analysis can involve a few hours as part of an educational program offered by a cosmetic company, or several days in a targeted course for a more customized approach.

Another challenge for the image consultant is mastering the language of color—learning to describe colors in many different ways in order to help your client see and experience what your trained eye sees. One person may respond to color by the technical terms you use, and another through poetic, artistic descriptions. As a consultant, your job is to identify which approach is most effective for your client.

Direct Selling and Trunk Shows

A lucrative way to increase revenues as an image consultant is to represent and sell a product line through a direct selling company. Trunk shows were common in the frontier days when traveling salesmen sold their merchandise out of a trunk. *Trunk show* is a term commonly used among modern designers who show their couture collections in stores for a week: "Come meet the designer at the ABC Store and see the Trunk Show."

"If the shoe fits, you're not allowing for growth."
—Robert N. Coons

Companies like Doncaster, French Rags, Juliana Collezione, Worth, and Carlisle provide training to the consultant in product knowledge and sales. The product is often unique and only available through the consultant, not in stores or catalogues.

Direct selling companies today have capitalized on the benefits of convenience and personalized service. The image consultant also benefits from the direct selling approach. She has at her disposal a product line without the investment of a large inventory. In addition, she has an opportunity to earn revenues from commissions within specific weeks of the year. This way of working is ideal for a person who wants part-time business. The product line brings ample opportunity to attract new customers and attract new markets. For some consultants, handling and selling a product may not be as threatening as a personal service, and therefore easier to sell and generate revenue.

One of the challenges to direct selling occurs when too many consultants sell the same line in a small geographic region. For example, if more than one consultant belongs to the same golf club, client lists are bound to overlap. Be sure to research the commitment the company has to its consultants and its policies on customer service, delivery dates, and commissions. Most importantly, select a product line that you can be excited to work with and wear.

Bridal Consulting

Some image consultants work strictly on weddings and wedding events. The scope of their work can vary from choosing the dresses to taking on the role of project manager or coordinator for the whole series of events leading up to the wedding.

As the event coordinator for a wedding, an image consultant plans with the bride and her parents every detail with the goal of achieving the desired image and ambiance for the wedding. Details such as flower arrangements, color schemes, wedding and bridesmaid dresses, outfits for the family, menswear, table settings, makeup and hairstyles, event locations, coordination with hotels, food selection, church flowers, care and accommodations for guests, limousines and transportation, travel and honeymoon arrangements, and trousseau and honeymoon clothes can all fall within the role of the consultant. For a big wedding, an image consultant is likely to have a staff or a team and would undoubtedly need many local and business community resources from which to draw.

The qualities needed to do this kind of work successfully are many and varied. The consultant needs to have an enormous capacity for detail, the ability to keep many plates in the air at once, a knack for calling on resources and help, a cool head, empathy and compassion for people who are emotional and stressed, excellent crisis and time management skills, and the ability to carry the big vision at all times.

Fashion Feng Shui

An emerging dimension of image consulting is called Fashion Feng Shui. A holistic approach, Fashion Feng Shui incorporates the basic Feng Shui principles of arrangement and placement of objects to create optimum *chi,* or life energy, in one's surroundings. Although Feng Shui has traditionally been used in architecture and design, image consultants trained in Feng Shui have translated and transferred these principles to personal appearance, clothing design, and wardrobe analysis. The approach integrates a variety of principles and methods of individual assessment and applies them to clothing and wardrobe planning.

Using the language of Feng Shui's five life-forming elements—water, wood, fire, earth, and metal—Fashion Feng Shui facilitators translate color, design, and line into energetic components in order to make wardrobe choices that harmonize with the energy of both the wearer and his or her environment.

The philosophy of Fashion Feng Shui maintains that wearing clothing not in harmony with our personal *chi* may negatively affect the energy of the wearer and even other people's perceptions of the wearer, thus negatively influencing the experience and effectiveness of the relationship. Therefore, Fashion Feng Shui's intention is to create harmony at both the visual and experiential level. Additionally Fashion Feng Shui facilitators apply the principles of order, energy, and flow to closet organization and wardrobe planning.

Image Consultants Who Serve Organizations

A corporate image consultant offers a varied menu of seminars and workshops. At the beginning of your career you might confine yourself to just image and nonverbal communication or etiquette or presentation skills. More often than not, however, you will be asked to train people in a number of skills pertaining to image and professional presence. As your confidence grows and you build on your own education, you will be able to offer an increasing number of courses and programs. One rule of thumb in the image consulting business is to be a lifelong learner. New and updated skills always increase your value to an organization, not to mention bolster your own self-confidence.

Corporate clients may request training programs or presentations for segments of their staff. They might also require the consultant to work with individuals within the organization. Programs for groups are called *workshops, keynote presentations, training sessions,* or *lunch and learn programs.* They may be a featured single event or part of a larger corporate event. An extended management or sales training session, trade show, conference, or association convention would fall into this category. In some ideal situations, your program may be a regular and integral part of a company's management training courses or new-hire orientations.

Topics addressed in corporate or association programs may include:

- Dressing for success and internal career advancement
- Communication and conflict resolution skills
- Nonverbal and verbal skills
- Customer service
- Grooming and hygiene
- Business protocol and social etiquette
- International etiquette
- Networking
- Self-esteem
- Presentation and podium skills
- Interviewing techniques

"Always continue your own journey of personal development. Only then will you become a master-ul image consultant."
—*Jon Michail, AICI*

40

- Business casual dress
- Telephone skills
- Business travel packing
- Cross-cultural and gender communications
- Corporate identity building
- Interpersonal effectiveness and relationship building

The items on this list are subject to change as workplace needs shift and evolve.

One thing that is certain in the corporate environment is that the more the client pays, the more the client expects in return for the image consulting investment. If you are being compensated well for your services, the client—deservedly so—will be demanding of your time and expect excellent program materials and delivery techniques. Your personal image should be appropriate to the organization that hires you. You may need to have numerous meetings, write formal proposals and outlines, and execute needs assessments before you close the deal. The corporate image consultant should also be prepared to wait to be paid, as many organizations are on disbursement cycles that are not designed to correspond to or support your personal cash flow needs. If you are good at building rapport and trained in needs assessment and communication skills, you may enjoy a lengthy relationship with your corporate clients as an adjunct consultant to their staff, particularly when you can offer many varied programs and ongoing professional development coaching to individuals or groups.

Keynote Speakers

Being a keynote speaker can be a highly paid activity in a consulting practice and is frequently an offshoot of your training work in corporations. Public speaking skills are different, however, from training and consulting skills. To be a successful and sought-after speaker, you need to deliver a strong message in an entertaining fashion. You must be entertaining and informative. You should be able to move, touch, and inspire people with the power of your words. You need to practice and polish your speaking skills, develop and craft your topics, and learn how to develop stories and humor as an integral part of your speech. As a speaker, you do not have the same feedback from your audience as you would in a classroom. Developing theater techniques is important, calling on many of the same techniques an actor would use to deliver a speech in a play.

Consultants are often asked to speak when they have written a book or published an article. A book serves as a very useful calling card and can definitely move you to the next level in the speaking profession. Join the National Speakers' Association or your local chapter and learn invaluable tricks and techniques of the trade. Toastmasters is also an excellent training ground to practice the rudiments of the speaking profession, or look for a class or courses in acting and theater techniques. A presentation coach can also be a wonderful help to develop your skills in this area.

When you are a keynote speaker, you must prepare well the delivery of your chosen subject. When you are teaching anything to a group, your knowledge, experience, and background will be challenged far more than information you give to an individual client. Your audience expects you to know anything and everything about your area of expertise, and image covers a variety of subjects! Not only will you be asked questions about the content of your talk, but you may also be asked about other material you have not included, or with which you are not familiar. Teaching a group demands a certain mastery of your subject. You will need a strong background and a depth of subject matter in your field before you attempt to teach anyone but a group of beginners.

Media Training

Consultants who perform media training work with high-level corporate employees, politicians and their families, and anyone who has to step into the public eye, face journalists, or appear on radio or television. Authors and corporate executives often employ a media coach when they have to represent their work or organization in public. Image consultants stress emphasizing the content of the message to be expressed; the style in which the message is to be spoken; and the nonverbal language, the subtext, and the appearance of the speaker. Media training requires an understanding of how makeup colors, clothing tones, and fabric textures and patterns behave on camera and under lighting. Media trainers often have a public speaking background, a thorough grounding in performance and communication skills on television and radio, and sometimes an acting background also.

Fashion Show Production

This field is ideal for the image consultant who wants to find a niche. You will need to be good at theatrical production and enjoy hectic organization, as well as have a grasp of current fashion and trends. Provincial mall and in-store fashion shows are not the lavish productions they once were because of escalating costs. In fact, many of the big stores do not put on fashion shows at all. As entertainment for fundraisers and women's groups, however, fashion shows are always popular. An educational fashion show—where a consultant can teach image principles as well as fashion trends—is an effective mix and an excellent way for the consultant to showcase her talents and gain some clients. You would align with a charity, an existing civic group, or an association and then obtain the clothes from one or more of the local boutiques, designers, or big stores.

Producing a fashion show presents many challenges, not the least of which is the work involved in hiring and fitting models, choreographing the show, and cleaning up after it is all over. Attention must be paid to the condition of the clothes and accessories and the problem of transporting everything to the venue. If fine jewelry or high-priced items are involved, hire a security guard . The biggest challenge is the organization of the show itself. Both backstage and onstage segments of a fashion show must receive equal attention. The wise image consultant enlists the aid of either a backstage organizer or master of ceremonies to help divide and organize the workload into manageable segments.

Image Consultants Who Are Permanent Corporate Employees

Personal Shopper

An in-house *personal shopper* employed by a major retailer serves the individual client in much the same way as her independent counterpart, with some important differences. First, the in-house shopper is usually on a draw against commission sales and therefore dependent only upon the sales of the clothes for income. Occasionally she draws a set salary and receives no commission. Second, the in-house consultant may not have the exposure to the client's needs (lifestyle, current wardrobe, and budget parameters). Third, this type of employee is limited to servicing the client with whatever choices are available in the store. Advantages to being an in-house personal shopper include health insurance and other corporate benefits. Employment as an in-house personal shopper is also a wonderful training ground to find out if you like the job of image consulting, before committing to your own entrepreneurial venture.

An in-house image consultant might be asked to produce in-store fashion shows—hiring the models and arranging the whole event. She may also be required to put on free seminars for local organizations as a way of marketing her services and the store to the community. Nordstrom, Neiman-Marcus, Saks Fifth Avenue, and other high-end stores and boutiques are the most likely to set up a personal shopping service.

Corporate Image Consultant

The in-house consultant to a corporation may provide the employee population with the same services as his independent counterpart. This consultant may be part of the Human Resources, Training and Development, or Sales and Customer Services departments, and therefore must comply with the specific needs and expectations of these departments. An image consultant considering taking an in-house corporate job must weigh and assess the employee benefits: regular paycheck and political climate of the job against the freedom of owning one's own business. Actually, very few organizations hire staff image consultants. The Disney corporations, a few universities, and perhaps a financial institution or two come to mind.

College Facilitators

Another nonentrepreneurial image expert is one who teaches or organizes image consulting courses at fashion colleges or teaches image skills to students in other capacities. Many fashion schools are now offering image consulting courses, and many colleges and higher education institutions are offering programs for interviewing skills. These programs include advice on dress, appearance, resume writing, interview techniques, and communication skills. Continuing Education Institutes and some government agencies also offer similar programs for a wide range of candidates who are seeking employment yet lack the image skills necessary to land a job.

Challenges for All Categories of Image Consulting

As image consultants, we are expected to offer our clients advice. The difference between the advice of an image consultant and that of an interior decorator or lawyer is that the image consultant may seem to be challenging someone's *personal opinion* in style, dress, accessories, and hair. Unsolicited critiques are sometimes interpreted as criticism. Since image is such a personal subject, an image consultant needs to make sure that the client/ subject really wants to hear the critique.

One way of ensuring commitment on the part of the client is to arrange a paid session. Another method is to work with someone who has publicly volunteered himself or herself in a group or class. In either scenario, the critiques must take a positive, constructive stance, separating appearance issues from the actual individual. For example, you would concentrate on fit or camouflage techniques rather than pointing obviously to a person's weight gain or figure challenge, which may already be a sensitive issue.

When your presentation is offered as education, the risk of the client feeling judged is minimized or even eliminated. Remember that your recommendations should be based upon sound image principles, not your personal opinion. Everyone has opinions, but as a professional image consultant, you are expected to bring an objective expertise to the situation. Another excellent strategy is to link your critique to the client's goals. For example, you could indicate how a new image can enhance her self-confidence or advance her career.

CHAPTER FOUR

What Image Consulting Skills Do You Need?

To provide broad image consulting services to individuals from both the private and corporate sector requires skills, knowledge, and mastery in most, if not all, aspects of image. Image is an umbrella under which falls the spectrum of appearance and personal image communications. The Association of Image Consultants International, through extensive research and evaluation, has identified and developed a core curriculum. This list shows basic skills that you should have to start an image consulting business. At the beginning of your career, you will need a broad background and must become proficient in many of the topics listed in the basic core curriculum. As you grow and perhaps specialize, you will require a higher level of mastery in the areas in which you advertise your expertise.

"Apply yourself. Ge all the education you can, but then, by Go do something. Don' just stand there, mal it happen."
—Lee Iacocca

Technical Image Skills

If you are an image consultant whose business focus is basic image consulting to individuals, you will most likely be offering color analysis, wardrobe assessments and closet audits, personal shopping, and wardrobe planning. In order to perform and deliver these services, you will need to have foundation skills in:

- Color analysis
- Body and line analysis
- Basic design principles, such as balance, proportion, scale, and harmony
- Wardrobe construction
- Fabrications and textiles
- Wardrobe planning, selection, and coordination strategies

- Cost and budget assessment for your client's level
- Lifestyle evaluation to identify what needs the client has, such as interviews, promotion, dating, and traveling
- Fashion trends, current events, and lifestyle trends
- Fashion and other resources
- Accessories coordination and resources
- Consulting techniques

If you want to work with both men and women, you will need to be knowledgeable in menswear and women's wear. Menswear places a much greater emphasis on the construction, fit, fabric, style, and subtle use of pattern than does women's wear.

Communication Skills

In order to communicate effectively with your clients, you will need a basic understanding of customer signals (body language, nonverbal messages, open or closed responsiveness, and so on), listening skills, personality types, and communication styles. Business etiquette and protocol are essential skills for knowing how to behave in a business atmosphere. You may also need to make adjustments when your clients are from various social strata and ethnically diverse backgrounds. An appreciation of basic psychology will take you a long way in this business. Communicating with men may require a different style than communicating with women. The image and wardrobe needs of a conservative executive woman are obviously different from those of a musical performing artist. Image consultants are expected to tackle any assignment that comes their way, or refer the business to someone else.

Business Skills

To maintain the operations of your business you will need to have basic entrepreneurial skills for marketing and growing your consulting practice. This list includes:

- Goal setting and planning
- Time management and priority setting

"If people don't want to listen to you, what makes you think they want to hear from your sweater?"
—Fran Lebowitz

- Business writing skills
- Speaking skills to communicate with prospects, clients, and small groups
- Business math for cash flow management
- Sales, marketing, and networking skills to attract clients to you
- Technological computer skills to develop your materials and maintain client lists on a database

If, in the assessment, you scored low in the business skills you can conceivably hire professionals and coaches to perform some of these tasks or teach you the skills. At first, you will discover that it is in your best interest to master your own business skills. Doing so will enable you to be more independent and increase your profits. Later in your career, you might delegate the tasks at which you are less proficient while you continue to grow in the areas in which you are interested and are likely to excel.

Personal Image

Your own image should be exemplary. You should look like an image consultant. You must demonstrate an attention to detail, a love of color, and an appreciation of fabric and design. You will need a well-designed haircut in a fashionable style and an attractive color. Your makeup should be well applied and blended. Since you must appeal to a wide variety of people, your image should not be so faddish that you scare most people away. Your shoes should be well polished, your hose run-free, and your garments clean and well-groomed. You should know how to wear clothes to their best advantage: fashionable without being freakish, in good taste without being boring.

Consulting and Training Skills

If you intend to work with the corporate sector to provide consulting programs, coaching, seminars, and workshops to groups within an organization, be prepared to increase your level of mastery in all the foundation skills. The corporate client's expectations are much higher and more demanding. You will have to learn educational methods and group exercises and skills to engage the whole group at one time, in order to keep their interest. You must also have the ability to teach each skill simply, for people who do not have your level of expertise, and to break down the topic so that participants can grasp the concept and be able to use it themselves.

In addition to the basic image consultant's skills, you will also need to be well-versed in the skills required to teach groups, and possess a basic knowledge of how an organization operates. For teaching and training you must:

- Perform needs assessments to identify the objectives of the program
- Develop a curriculum or program outline to meet their needs and your objectives
- Understand group dynamics and the learning process
- Be familiar with some communication, learning, and interpersonal effectiveness methodologies such as neurolinguistic programming, personality profiles, or brain dominance styles
- Make a collection of teaching games, exercises, and role-play methods to engage the audience
- Develop or acquire presentation materials, workbooks, visuals, and a PowerPoint presentation
- Be comfortable with question-and-answer techniques

- Know training etiquette and business protocol
- Develop excellent speaking skills
- Understand the hierarchical structure and politics within an organization
- Gather a basic understanding of organizational development and team or group dynamics

Depending upon your program topics, you may also need to master the following in order to teach them effectively:

- Professional business etiquette and protocol
- Image communications, perception management, strategic dressing
- Customer service
- Verbal and presentation skills, telephone skills, listening and speaking techniques
- Nonverbal and body language skills
- Business casual dress
- Business trends in the workplace

AICI Core Curriculum & Related Topics

A basic core curriculum is a course of study or background of information which supports the development of all image professionals at all levels, regardless of specialty, enabling a diverse membership base. It defines the minimum universal requirements for image professionals as a foundation to an extensive, ongoing process of learning that builds the skills, knowledge, and experience necessary for continuous productivity, growth, and business success.

Image

Appearance		
Personal	**Wardrobe Management**	**Apparel**
Hair	Quality Factors	Principles of Design
Cosmetics	Fit Factors	Elements of Design
Skin care	Alterations/Custom Clothing	Fashion Coordination
Nail care	Cost & Budget Factors	Fashion Trends & Forecasting
Fragrance	Wardrobe Evaluation/Closet	Fashion History
Dental care	Audit	Functions of Apparel
Nutrition	Closet Organization	Psychology of Fashion
Grooming	Wardrobe Planning	Sociology of Fashion
Fitness	Accessorizing	Influence of Image
Poise	Personal Shopping	Fabrications & Textiles
Cosmetic Surgery	Body Analysis	Garment Construction
Personal Color Analysis	Personal Body Style Selection	Color Harmony
Body & Line analysis	and Coordination	Print, Pattern, Texture
Balance, Proporation, Scale	Personality Selection/	
Face Shapes, Line Direction, &	Coordination	
Line Movement	Personal Color Selection and	
	Coordination	
	Personal Lifestyle Selection	
	and Coordination	
	Special-Interest-Group Needs	
	Dress Code Guidelines	
	Development	

Behavior		
Personality	**Social**	**Corporate**
Self-Esteem	International Protocol	Customer Service
Self-Concepts	Social Etiquette	Dress Code
Perceptions, Attitudes, Beliefs	Event Planning	Business Etiquette
Individual Identity	Cultural Awareness	Corporate Climate
Group Identity	Social Styles	Coaching/Consulting
Personal Values, Ethics, Goals		
Lifestyle Management		

Communications

Presentation	Interpersonal	Public
Verbal	Conflict Resolution	Public Relations
Vocal	Leadership	Media
Visual	Team Building	Materials Development
Body Language	Listening	Public Speaking
Writing	Negotiating	Teaching/Training
Communication Styles	Interviewing	
	Networking	

Business

Development and Management

Niche	Promotion	OrganizationApparel
Target Markets	Identity Package	Business Plan
Product Development	Promotional Materials	Objectives
Service Development	Web Site	Goals
Setting Fees	Media Kit	Mission Statement
Location & Setup	Advertisements	Corporate Identity
Future Growth	Referral Sources	30-second Commercial
	Strategic Alliances	Standards
	Cross Promotion	Culture/Philosophy
	Networking	Organizational Chart
	Direct Mail	
	Newsletters E-zines/E-mail	
	Telemarketing	
	Follow-up	

Electronic Equipment

Promotional Materials	Presentation Materials	Office
Web Page Setup and Design	PowerPoint	Computer Software
Internet Selling	Visual Aids	Computer Hardware
Internet Research	Audio Aids	

Functions

Administration	Operations	Marketing
Social/Economic Trends	Personal Skills	Public Relations
Analysis	Inventory Control	Sales & Service
Strategic Planning	Adult Learning Concepts	Advertising
Support Systems	Development Content and	Display/Merchandising
Strategic Alliances	Format	
Professional Associations	Teaching Methods	
Accounting/Bookkeeping	Consulting Methods	
Financing & Fundraising	Coaching Methods	
	Needs Assessment Procedures	
	Evaluations Development	
	Follow-up Methods	

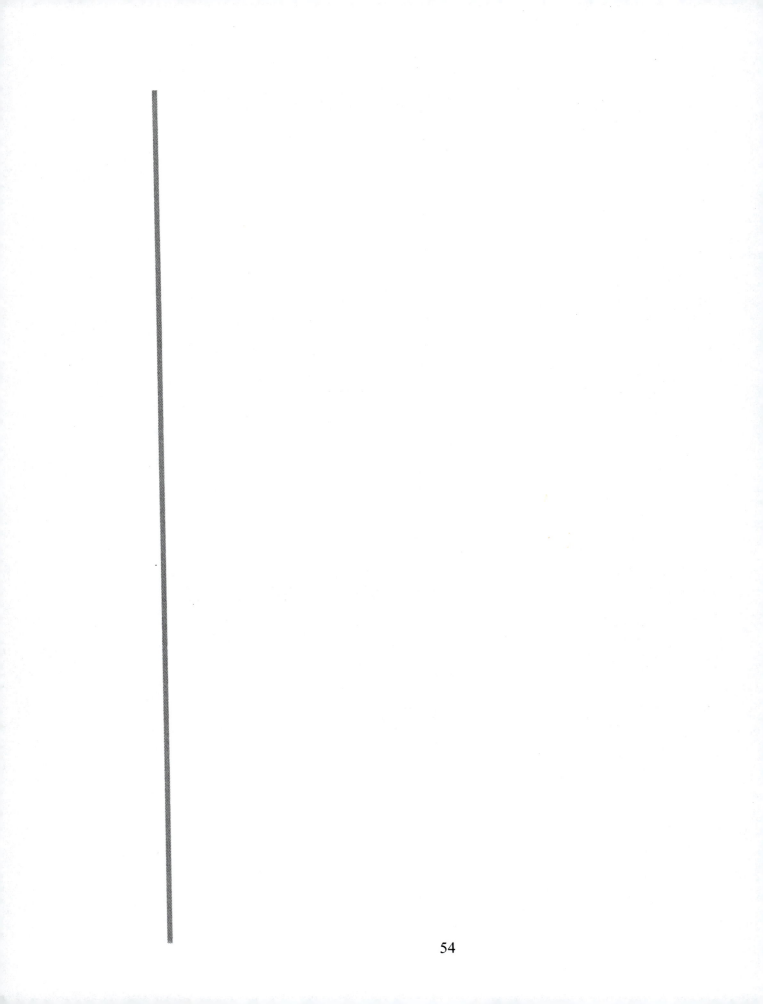

CHAPTER FIVE

What Can You Expect to Earn?

To answer the question of what you can expect to earn as an image consultant, we must ask you to answer a few additional questions, because the answer is actually: *It depends.*

Your compensation will depend upon

- Your level of experience and expertise
- The actual services you offer, including single services or packages
- Your geographic region
- Your costs of doing business
- Your clients' expectations
- Your target market, i.e., specialty niche, high end, mass market

The more experience, training, and credibility you have, the higher the fee you can command. The more metropolitan and cosmopolitan your market, the more the client will be willing to pay for a high-quality person who can deliver high-quality products and services.

The individual clients and corporate training professionals who hire you can often discern your true level of experience. Today's clients research the people they choose to hire. Your best approach is to underpromise and overdeliver. Your value to the client should be higher than he is expecting. If you make this a rule, you will be able to go back to clients for testimonials and referrals and enjoy long-term, professional relationships.

"Profit is the product of labor plus capital multiplied by management. You can hire the first two. The last must be inspired."
—*Fost*

What you charge is one part of the equation. The second is your costs of doing business. In later chapters, we address some typical business scenarios and compare your costs to your revenues. If your costs are high, then you must absolutely do a cost-of-service analysis with an analysis of your target market in order to know your breakeven point and your profit potential.

Annual Income Ranges of Image Consultants

In a 1999 survey of members of the Association of Image Consultants International, respondents reported deriving most of their income from personal consultations, corporate seminars, and product sales. The survey asked for the members' most recent annual income from image consulting. The responses were as follows:

Under $10,000	2%
$10,000–$24,999	17%
$25,000–$49,999	22%
$50,000–$99,999	25%
$100,000–$199,999	11%
Over $200,000	3%
Starting out	13%
Part-time	38%
Full-time	49%

The annual income ranges are as follows for people working full-time who fall into one of the three primary categories of image consultants (individual clients, corporate clients, or in-house staff):

Personal Shopper $15,000–$110,000

(Hourly fees and/or commissions; includes

people whose business is direct selling)

Full-Service Image Consultant $25,000–$150,000

(Offering color analysis, products, shopping,

wardrobe services, and some group presentations)

Corporate Image Consultant $30,000–$150,000

Working for an Organization $20,000–$75,000
(In-house personal shopper; in-house image
consultant/trainer)

To start calculating how much you can earn, look at the table of fees on page 62. The matrix displays examples of several ranges of fees and rates taken from many information sources nationwide. To start projecting how much money you can make as an image consultant, consider the fees you can charge for different services you provide and factor in the number of clients to whom you can reasonably provide these services.

Modes of Compensation

Charging Hourly Rates

Consultants working with individuals (for both corporations and private clients) often charge by the hour. Look at the financial rates matrix on page 60 to see the range into which you would fall.

First, you need to calculate your hourly worth as determined by your total professional experience, your image experience, and your geographical region. The advantage to charging by the hour is that the meter is running as long as you are working for your client. You can easily calculate your billable hours, and the clients can feel in control as they know they can start or stop the meter as they work with you, provided that there are some guiding parameters. How many hours a week do you expect to be able to bill? If your rate is $100 per hour and you work four hours one week, three another, two the third week, and five hours the fourth week, then your gross earnings are $1,400 for that month.

Sometimes you can also charge for research and travel time. Make sure that these costs are clearly indicated and understood by the client. You must also factor in your costs of materials and either build payment for them into your fee structure or charge extra. Take, for example, the color analysis personal swatch palette. If you pay $10 to $20 for this item, then you need to factor in an additional cost to the client.

Charging by the Package, Project, or Job

If you offer a package rate, list exactly what your package includes. For example, a home wardrobe and closet analysis package may include:

- Analysis of the client's body line, fit, and clothing shape
- Fashion style, and an assessment of the current season's wardrobe
- Wardrobe strategy for the client's upcoming situations
- Accessory integration and outfit creation
- Personal shopping game plan, identifying any wardrobe gaps

Determine how long the service will take you to provide and set your package rate. You might consider taking less per hour than you would if you were charging hourly rates to provide the customer with an incentive to buy a package, which guarantees you a certain amount of work. State up front that any extra services provided beyond those specified in the agreed-upon package will be billed at your normal hourly fee.

If your session looks as though it may require more time than you forecast, then about 30 minutes before the budgeted ending time, you should reassess with your client. At this time you should agree on priorities, address those, and ask the client if she is willing to extend the session at your hourly rate. The client then has the responsibility of choosing how she wishes to spend her time and budget. As a precaution, practice to make sure you know how much time it will take you realistically to complete the assignment. In the case of a shopping session, if you are slow to research for your client and you do not charge for preshopping, then your hourly fee is considerably diluted in value. Dropping your fees to underbid another consultant or undercutting your time may get you the sale but maybe not the profit. Neither will those practices be of value to the client in the long term. Always seek the best value for you and your client and stand by your principles.

A package may include a series of sessions in order to offer a volume discount. Since image enhancement is truly a process, this approach can be most advantageous and realistic to the client. You will also benefit by providing a full and rewarding service. A series of sessions also serves as an incentive to the client to work through the process completely with you as her coach. Package or volume discounts always help the client feel as if she is receiving something of great value for less money. Work out the number of hours a client will need from you per season and then work out a realistic yearly or seasonal total. You can also offer a discount to clients who pay the entire amount for the package up front, which saves them money and puts cash into your pocket.

Daily Rates

Corporate clients customarily pay image consultants by the day. They may then schedule hourly sessions for you with their staff members. Private clients may also prefer to pay a day rate; you can offer a slight discount to the client in this case, too, as you are assured of earning a minimum amount for the designated period of time. You should be able to clarify expectations so that the client knows exactly what comes with the day rate. You might include in the daily rate amounts for materials, your fee, travel time, research time, etc.— each listed but not charged separately.

Commissions and Percentages

Consultants who sell products—such as Doncaster, Carlisle, or Juliana Collezione clothing, cosmetics, and some accessories—may receive a commission on the sale of their products. These range from 30 percent to 50 percent depending on your volume. You may also have a financial arrangement with the stores and boutiques in your area. Commissions of 5 percent to 15 percent are typical and can be collected after each sale or in monthly or quarterly disbursements, depending on the initial arrangement. Sometimes arrangements can be made to barter commissions for clothes and other services.

Product Sales

Some consultants choose to sell a product such as clothing, jewelry, or cosmetics. The benefit of selling a product is that you have the potential of repeat sales, whereas with a service, the client may only need the color analysis once. In some cases, consultants who sell clothes may need to invest in an inventory of merchandise. In other cases, such up-front investment is not necessary. Marketing clothes can take a number of different forms. Consultants may sell the clothes with no extra services from a room or the basement of their house, or in conjunction with their services. They may even use the products as a way to interest clients in their services. The typical way to sell these designer collections is by issuing invitations to your home for a one-week show per season. People are invited to come and view the samples and then order selections.

In the case of makeup, consultants often include a makeover as part of the individual consultation, or set up small gatherings in homes and offices where all the women can experiment with the makeup and order at the end of the session. The consultant must purchase the items in advance, usually at wholesale or volume discount rates, and make a profit similar to a retail operation. The profit varies depending on the type of merchandise. Makeup and skin care—if purchased wholesale from a manufacturer, for example—may easily be marked up at least 100 percent, if not more. The success of this revenue center depends upon the intention. Is it to make a clear profit on the product sales or to use the product as a vehicle to interest new client prospects? At the very least, find a product that you are excited about and that you feel certain your type of client will want and need. A word of reality: inventory can easily tie up your cash flow if you cannot move it quickly.

If you are fortunate to work with some of the lesser-known designers in your area, then you may be able to obtain products on consignment. Only if you sell them are you obliged to pay the vendor their predetermined price. Sales from consignment merchandise may bring a lower profit margin, but you don't risk tying up your capital in inventory.

Retainers

A few corporate clients and even a few individual clients will pay you a retainer fee as their consultant. A retainer is an excellent way of planning your projected income by selling your services as an in-depth package or a series of sessions. For example, you offer 10 to 20 hours of consulting to an individual client for a package fee. If the work will take place over a period of months, you could request a monthly payment. Another way is to be paid a monthly fee towards a long-term project. With this fee structure, you have the benefit of being able to count on long-range income while still having the freedom of being your own boss. Knowing that you will be receiving a monthly check helps you project your cash flow.

Rules of Thumb for Compensation

- *The more you put into it, the more you can get out of it.*

- *Working smarter can bring a higher return than working harder.*

- *You can set your fees by observing the results you produce and their value to the client.*

The Financial Ranges Matrix

Individual Consulting (hourly ranges)

	Rural Areas	Medium to Small Towns	Large Metro Cities	Int'l Fashion Capitals *
Beginner 0-3 years experience & training	$25 - $50	$50 - $75	$50 - $100	$75 - $150
Intermediate 3-6 years experience	$50 - $75	$75 - $95	$75 - 100	$75 - $150
Experienced/ Advanced 6+ years	$75 - $95	$95 - $150	$150 - $200	$150 - $300

Corporate Image Consulting (approximate daily ranges)

	Rural Areas	Medium to Small Towns	Large Metro Cities	Int'l Fashion Capitals *
Beginner 0-3 years experience and/or training	$250 - $500	$500 - $1500	$500 - $1500	$750 - $2000
Intermediate 3-6 years experience	$250 - $1000	$500 - $1500	$750 - $2000	$1500 - $4500
Experienced/ Advanced 6+ years	$1000 - $2000	$1500 - $3000	$2000 - $6000	$3000 - $6000

Neither the authors nor AICI make any recommendation or endorsements of specific fees. The ultimate decision of fees and charges should be made by each independent consultancy.

* International fashion capitals such as New York, Tokyo, London, San Francisco or other global cities.

CHAPTER SIX

What Business Skills Do You Need?

If you have answered the assessment surveys honestly and to the best of your knowledge, you will end up with a score that reflects your aptitude for image consulting. Make a note of your gaps. To fill in those gaps, make plans to read, attend courses, take on a coach or delegate tasks to others to ensure that your business is well-rounded, with all the bases covered.

Entrepreneurial Skills

You need to be aware of the weight and spread of your scores. If you are high on the majority of the technical image skills but low on the business topics, and you know that you would find it difficult to sell or promote yourself, then you must question your aptitude to be the head of your own business. You will sometimes be selling yourself, your products, and your services to strangers over the phone, and you will have to distinguish yourself from any competitors. To some people this prospect is terrifying, while to others it poses no problem.

Business Writing

As a business owner you will need to market your company. You may need to write business communications such as flyers, letters, brochures, collateral materials, and proposals. Good writing and business communication skills are useful tools to acquire (or even barter), since hiring a professional to write everything for you can become expensive. Nothing erodes your professional image and credibility quicker than poorly written documents, riddled with spelling and grammatical errors and typos. Attend classes to improve these critical skills if necessary.

Basic Business Skills

Time management and office organization are basic business skills, the lack of which pose problems for any professional. Clients hire you the first time for your talents or reputation as a consultant or speaker, but repeat business is earned. If you are competent, keep to your schedule, arrive on time, return calls in a timely manner, and appear ready to work to the exclusion of other distractions, you will likely be asked again to perform your services. However good you are as an image professional, these nonverbal image builders are as important as your professional talents, and they greatly enhance your image to clients.

Office and Organizational Systems

As your business grows so will your administrative workload. Having systems to deal with your increased workload before you need them is an essential preventive measure for administrative avalanches. What if, for instance, your successful marketing efforts produce excellent results, and you end up with more business than you can handle? You may also find yourself overloaded because of unexpected deadlines; family distractions such as illness, vacations, and holidays; unrealistic time management or unscheduled interviews; and crises that require immediate attention. Perhaps your business has busy seasons. For these challenges, seasonal or otherwise, you must absolutely plan ahead. Do not overfill your schedule. If you know you will be busy or time will be at a premium, make sure you give yourself extra time between appointments for your preparatory work.

Ruthlessly differentiate items that are urgent from those that are important. Items that are unimportant, yet seem to sneak to the top of your priority to-do list, are dangerous. For example, a client calls you from a store desiring feedback on her potential purchases and needs you to respond immediately. Meanwhile, you have a corporate client waiting for a proposal, which—if you do not get it in on time—may cost you your next month's rent. You need to be able to differentiate the urgent from the important, and choose your actions accordingly. This principle guides you to make choices based upon a clear understanding of the impact and reaction to your actions. In both of Stephen Covey's books, *The Seven*

Habits of Highly Effective People and *First Things First*, he clearly explains how to sort these types of tasks by placing them into quadrants or priority order. Wasted and lost time is ultimately lost money.

One way to save time and money is to have a processing system for all the activities and functions of your business. For example, consider how you will process a person from the initial inquiry call to becoming a client. One routing suggestion is to have a form to record the client's information (see sample in appendix). It should contain a place to write all the contact information, nature of the client's need, objectives for that client, what must be sent or e-mailed to the client, conversation triggers (particular words the client used), time frame of need (with due date), and follow-up suggestions. If you have a multifaceted business, you may want a separate, color-coded inquiry form for each category of client: yellow for media inquiries, client inquiries in blue, and corporate program inquiries in white, for example. The information from your forms can be keyed into a database. If you are like many image consultants, you are juggling multiple tasks. It is easy to write a quick note to yourself, and later on forget what the note was for. A free-flowing information system will ultimately save you many hours, and perhaps some clients.

You need to determine what information about your clients you want to track. If personal shopping is a big part of your business, you will need a constantly updated resource list of vendors, suppliers, stores, and boutiques for every income level. If you do corporate training, then you will need to keep up-to-date on learning trends in the workplace, business communication tools such as DiSC, coaching tools, and the latest teaching videos.

A system for following up on your leads is also essential. Without such a system to prompt you, good leads can quickly disappear. Every lead is a potential client; it might be someone you met personally, on-line, or at the grocery store, or the lead may be a referral from a networking group or client. After you record the information about the lead, you should have a sequence of follow-up steps—for example,

- Recording the contact information
- Sending an information packet
- Following up with a phone call

Then, after initial attempts at follow-up, consider your subsequent moves:

- If you did not make contact at the first call, how many subsequent calls will you try?
- Will you set up an information-gathering meeting over breakfast, lunch, tea?
- How will you keep the lead in a marketing cycle—with a newsletter, flyer, or phone campaign?

Database Design and Use

A well-designed database can save you hours of wasted time and help you make money as a marketing support tool. Many software programs are available on the market, each of which has its benefits. Some have preset design templates, and some allow more customization. Find one that is user-friendly for your level of computer comfort and one that can grow as your business and database needs grow. If you are not skilled at the actual database design, seek the professional assistance of a coach or systems designer. This expense can save you valuable time and money in the long run. The design stage requires that you know and anticipate all the areas in which you will sort information (alphabetically, by occupation, gender, type of service used, prospect versus client, zip code, title, initial inquiry date, name of referral, and so on). You should be able to personalize communications through mail merges, as well as print out mailing labels, invoices, and summary reports. You will need to adapt your list for any of your marketing campaigns. For example, if you wanted to send a post card to all the prospective clients who contacted you in the past three months, you should be able to access their contact information with a few keystrokes.

Bookkeeping

The importance of well-organized financial records cannot be overemphasized. An accounting, bookkeeping, or software system should have the same characteristics of any other tool used in your business: sophisticated enough to serve your needs, yet simple enough for you to run it. Entrepreneurs often underestimate the amount of time needed to prepare a good set of financial records, and spend many hours catching up at tax time! Make sure that your record keeping is a high priority, preplanned and done on a consistent basis. As your business grows, you should work closely with your accountant or bookkeeper to ensure that your accounting system is appropriate for each stage of your business.

Questions to Ask Yourself When Setting Up a Record Keeping System

- How should you account for any inventory?
- What are fixed assets? Do you have any?
- What is your range of products and services and are they treated differently?
- Will you need to track accounts receivable?
- Will you do business in one or several states?
- What products or services are subject to sales tax?
- What type of government or state controls are you subject to?
- When do you file your business tax statements?
- Are you paying payroll taxes or do you have contract labor?

Your Business Structure

Your Legal Entity

The financial and legal aspects of your business are best outsourced to a professional accountant and lawyer who know your business and can serve as a network of support. The form of business entity you choose will determine your protection under the law and your income tax requirements.

Business organizations take one of three basic forms. In all cases, when starting your business you should seek legal counsel or the advice of a business-oriented accountant to ascertain which entity suits your situation.

Sole Proprietorship

Typically this type of business is owned and operated by one individual or a husband-and-wife team. The owner has possession of the business assets and is directly responsible for the debts and liabilities incurred by the business. For tax purposes, the income or loss of a sole proprietorship is combined with all other earnings of an individual. This type of entity does not have any particular operating regulations and only requires a business license or permit to open the doors.

Partnership, General or Limited

A partnership is a legal entity with its own rights and responsibilities. It can sign contracts, obtain trade credit, and borrow money. A partnership is also required to file income tax returns, but the information is combined with the personal income of the partners to determine overall tax liability. Losses and profits are passed on to the partners' personal tax returns.

In a general partnership, two or more individuals join together to run a business enterprise. Each partner owns the company assets, is responsible for liabilities, and has authority to run the business—all of which can be appropriated by partnership agreement. Creditors also have recourse to the personal assets of each of the partners to settle debts.

A limited partnership is comprised of one or more general partners and one or more limited partners. General partners are personally liable for debts and take an active role in running operations. Limited partners contribute capital, share in profits and losses, do not take part in running the business, and may not be liable for the debts.

A word of advice: partnerships that are not well documented in writing are subject to memory losses and disagreements. All agreements should be in writing at the beginning of the enterprise or whenever a new agreement is reached and even signed. This formality will cut down (but not totally eliminate) any miscommunications and upsets, which may have dangerous repercussions on the personal relationships involved as well as the business itself.

Corporation

A corporate structure protects—under the "corporate veil"—the owners or shareholders from the liabilities of the business. The corporation is a distinct legal entity, existing on its own and separate from the individual(s) who own it. As such, the business will exist on its own even after the death of its owners. Corporations must also file income tax returns and pay taxes on income derived from the operations. Your corporation (you) must apply to the Secretary of State in your state to gain permission to do business. You then file articles of incorporation and by-laws, which govern the company's rights and obligations to shareholders, directors, and officers. Benefits of forming a corporation include liability protection, allowing an individual to sell or transfer one's interest in the business with ease, and providing continuity in the event that the business is sold. When you incorporate, a name search is performed. You then reserve and have the exclusive use of that business name.

Sub Chapter S Corporation

A sub chapter S corporation receives special treatment under the tax laws, being taxed as a partnership, with certain exceptions. For the first three to five years, you are taxed personally on the losses or profits of the sub S company. You are still protected from personal liabilities. Another reason for choosing this structure is to minimize the potential of double taxation on corporate income.

Each of these business structures has pros and cons. You can change your business structure after you have been in operation for a time, but expect such a change to cost money. We urge you, therefore, to consult with legal and financial counsel for the smartest structure for your circumstances and business goals. This action will save you time, worries, and money in the long run. Don't rush into a structure without doing your homework, as the decision about your form of business impacts the way you conduct your business, your risk factor, and your record keeping requirements.

Business License

The license to operate your business comes from the city or county where the business is located. If you are located inside your city limits, you would apply to city hall. If you are outside the corporate city limits, then apply to your county clerk's office. The license fee depends on the jurisdiction and the size of your business.

No special licenses or permits are currently required for an image consulting business. Check that your state allows the hands-on application of makeup, because state laws differ. Check also with your state cosmetology associations for any necessary license and training. Membership to a professional association such as AICI does not require licensing, but ongoing training is required to maintain the high professional standards of consultants in the profession. Training and AICI membership both provide competitive marketing advantages for you.

Home-Based Business versus an Office or Studio

As an image consultant you have several choices of work location available to you. If your work is primarily with individual clients in their homes or if you intend to become a personal shopper, you do not necessarily need a studio or an office outside the home. You could organize an area or a room in your house with a separate phone line, desk, computer, and fax. If you intend to work as a corporate trainer and will do your work inside the company, you can still keep your office at home. Many fashion consultants who carry lines of clothing show them to the best advantage in a room of their house.

Home-based businesses have benefits, aside from the obvious financial advantages of saving money on rent and being able to use the office-in-home tax deduction. Look closely at the way you work and your lifestyle. At home you can always fit in work at odd hours of the day and night. You are better able to arrange family activities and children's needs around your working hours. Many people who work at home find mixing work and home life easier.

Many consultants start their businesses at home and then later move to an outside location when their clientele is more established. A studio or an office space offers different advantages. Consultants report that they feel much more professional and believe that clients perceive them as more professional when they have an outside location. As a consultant, you can also keep your makeup line, color swatches, or products out on permanent display, as well as establish the most effective lighting and create an ambiance that best represents your company identity. Some consultants feel more motivated to succeed because of the financial commitment that is automatically built in every month. People who go out to work every day often find that they are able to separate work from home life more easily. When you lock the office door, you are finished for the day, and you can concentrate on another facet of your life.

Executive suites have also become quite popular. In this cooperative system, you pay a small monthly rent for communal services such as a receptionist and mail handling. You can then reserve room space at an hourly rate. A central receptionist can answer your calls, take messages, collect mail, and perform simple administrative tasks for your business.

When you want to use the office meeting rooms, you make a reservation for the time frame you need and pay only for those hours at a rate of approximately $10 - $50 per hour. (Regional rates vary.)

Ultimately, whether you rent space or work from home will depend on your own preferences and work style. If you are used to commuting to a place of work every day and do not work best with the distractions at home—but are terrified at the prospect of large monthly financial commitments—then you might consider sharing a space with another person, right from the start. Consultants have even been known to barter their space, giving image services in return for rooms in offices, beauty salons, or retail buildings. Necessity is often the mother of invention, and creative solutions to the stickiest problems can always be worked out or negotiated!

SECTION 2
How to Design Your Business

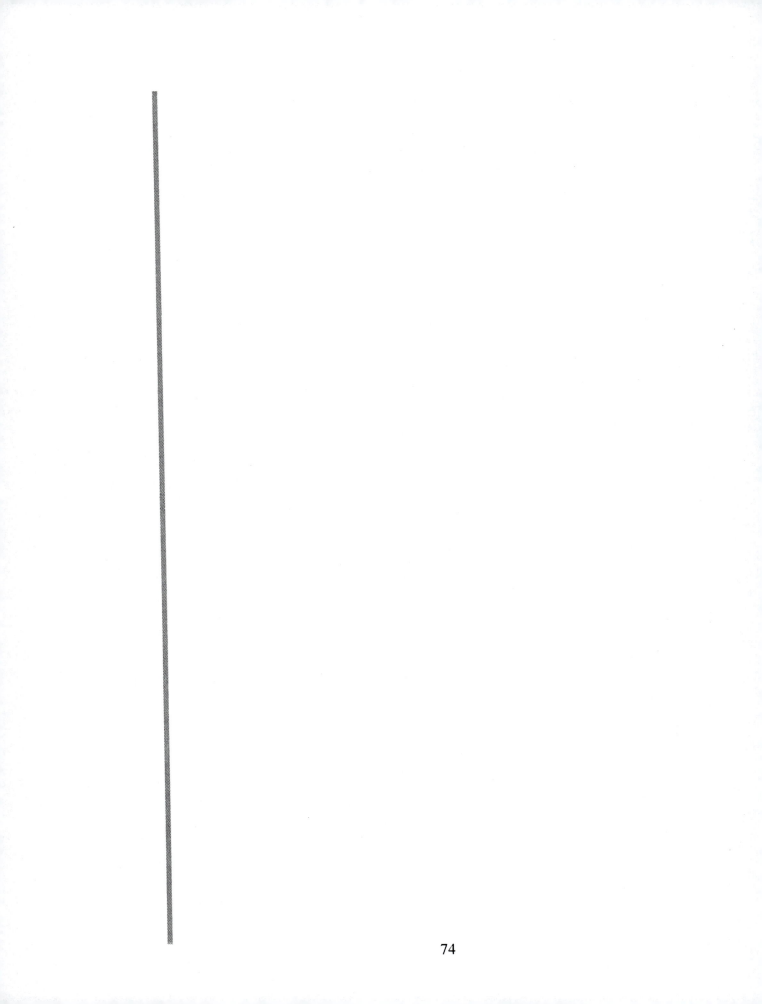

CHAPTER SEVEN

Creating Your Business Foundation with a Purpose and Vision

Whenever the word "vision" pops up in conversation, we always think of a dusty plaque on the wall with some platitudes that sound exactly the same as the last plaque on the last wall.

The vision on the plaque was brilliant at the time you or a group of people conceived the thought, and it was appropriate for the occasion. Now, however, the vision is frozen in time, its meaning having lost its immediate impact and the words retaining a somewhat "has-been" quality.

The question then becomes: why have a vision? Martin Luther King Jr. put it most succinctly. He stated: *"Man is man because he is free to operate within the framework of his destiny. He is free to deliberate, to make decisions and to choose between alternatives."* Human beings are capable of creating their own future. Doing so gives life a purpose, or as the French call it, a "raison d'être" (reason for being). When we have determined a meaning and a direction for our lives, business and personal decisions become much easier, career choices fall into place, and the possibility of living a life we love can become a reality.

Most pertinent to our fast-paced day-to-day activities is a vision as dynamic as we are, having applications in the moment, yet launching us into the future. We could choose words that galvanize us into action instantly—their power, *in the present tense,* able to recreate the forces that shape us in the future. In other words, we could have a dynamic vision for our lives that serves us moment by moment: A VISION-TO-GO, as it were! Instead of agonizing over the dilemmas of wordsmithing, or struggling to make the sentence sound eloquent or similar to all those other wall plaques, we could pick *words* or *phrases* that speak eloquently to us.

"If you don't stand for something, you'll fall for anything."
—Steve Bartkowski

In a vision the guiding principle is always based in the future: what do I want to be known for, and what contribution do I want to make? Think of words like truth, abundance, intuition, clarity, purpose, support, authenticity, bliss, joyful lives, contribution, outrageous future, creativity, empowerment, pioneering, honor, integrity, quality of life, human spirit, dignity, fulfillment, nurturing, generations to come, possibility, privilege, acknowledgment, excellence, breakthrough thinking, unimaginable, rejoice, magnificence. If at any time we wanted to make this sound professional (and plaque-worthy), we could fit the words into a sentence such as:

> **You can count on me** for inspiration, accomplishment, and authenticity as a team player.

> **Who I am** is excellence, enlightenment, love, and leadership.

> **What I stand for** is well-being, beauty, and creativity as the foundation of my image consulting business.

> **My company stands for** caring and powerful service, exceeding all expectations.

If we can have this outlook as a springboard for our lives, then we can also do it for our business, the day, the situation, the event, or even a conversation. If we took this approach on as a lifestyle, it would certainly give us a foundation on which to shape our attitude and dealings for the day. "Today I will take on truth, integrity, and loving life" seems a better thought to get out of bed with than "Thank God, It's Friday!" When we are in a financial crunch, let's adopt "abundance, serenity, and profound relationships" as a dynamic mindset and see how that might shift our current perspective of panic and scarcity.

It might take some work on our part to decide on these words, but with a little thought we can develop an instant vision bank. We could choose from a whole palette of words that represent the mood and attitude we select for what now becomes a life we create.

"The people who shape our lives and our cultures have the ability to communicate a vision or a quest or a joy or a mission."
—Anthony Robbins

Creating your Dynamic Vision

You could also select words appropriate to any situation at hand. You can have fun and use words that are outside the normal confines of the personality you have considered yourself to be.

If you are normally shy, you could choose "power, vitality, confidence, and self expression," for example, as the dynamic vision for your working life. If you know that you tend to be serious, try on "fun, unlimited, and playful relationships" for the working day. If life is a struggle, select words like "peace, ease, nurturing, making a difference, harmony, and contribution."

In the next series of exercises, take a moment to dwell on at least two of these questions. Answer the ones that speak loudest to you and that you have no difficulty answering.

- *What are your strengths?*

- *How would your coworkers or clients describe you?*

- *What can we count on you for?*

- *What do you want to be known for?*

- *What do you want your contribution to be in the world?*

Now, in regards to your career, take some of these questions and answer the ones that come naturally to you.

- *What is it about image consulting that you love most?*

- *When are you at your best doing this business?*

- *What are people attracted to you for?*

- *In what ways do people emulate you?*

- *What in this business is a totally natural fit and in what ways are you perfectly aligned with the job, where there is no struggle and effort?*

Write down your list of notes. You may be ready to select some words or phrases for your dynamic vision at this time. If not, ask a client or a coworker to tell you what contribution you make to their lives. Or simply let them tell you what your strengths are. Write down what they say and compare it to your notes. From all the data you have collected, find the common denominators. Select at least three words or phrases that inspire you and most creatively express your professional purpose or contribution in life. You can change these words at any time if you discover better ones. You can select words for your life purpose, your dynamic vision, or your consulting business. You could also select words appropriate to any situation at hand.

Let the words dictate the person you will be and what your contribution will be in life. You can also do this for your current project or situation. Try this daily for about two weeks, until you have a sense that this perspective is worthwhile and actually upgrades the caliber of your life. These words are not affirmations of your past, such as "reliable, good listener, hard worker." They are declarations of how you will contribute in the future and what you stand for despite circumstances or your current frame of mind. How would you like to be described at your memorial service? If you are inspired by something you have created, look at it weekly to see if it still represents your contribution. Make up others for the day, the project, or the next important interaction.

George Bernard Shaw expressed one of the most eloquent and inspiring visions when he accepted his Nobel Prize for literature.

> *"This is the true joy in life, the being used for a purpose recognized by yourself as being a mighty one: the being a force of nature instead of a feverish, selfish little clod of ailments and grievances complaining that the world will not devote itself to making you happy. I am of the opinion that my life belongs to the whole community, and as long as I live it is my privilege to do for it whatever I can. I want to be thoroughly used up when I die, for the more I create the more I live.*

I rejoice in life for its own sake. Life is no brief candle to me. It is a sort of splendid torch which I have got hold of for the moment, and I want to make it burn as brightly as possible before handing it on to future generations."

Sample Vision Statement

Consider the following vision statement for a hypothetical image consulting firm: *Image Company International is dedicated to self-discovery, beauty of expression, mastery, and loving life. We empower people to recognize their self-worth, to create and design their image as a powerful self-expression, and to nurture their communities through love, connectivity, collaboration, and communication.*

You can now have a "Dynamic Vision" for yourself and your business (and these could be the same). You can allow yourself to be totally inspired by it, therefore setting your goals in a different state of mind. Any time you are developing goals, first create the *dynamic vision* to inspire and motivate yourself. This exercise is even more effective if you do it in a dialogue with a friend, group, mentor, or partner. Once you have your vision, you are ready for action.

"I got the blues thinking of the future, so I left off and made some marmalade. It's amazing how it cheers one up to shred oranges and scrub the floor."
—D. H. Lawrence

Professional Goals

By reflecting on the following question, you will have a process to guide you in setting and realizing your goals: *What specific goals would you like to accomplish in the next month, quarter, and year?*

Write out your goals, and build a bit of a realistic stretch into them. A financial goal of $150,000 annual salary in the first year might not be realistic for an image start-up business. More realistic goals for just starting up might be: developing a brochure, gaining acceptance at three speaking bureaus, performing ten corporate seminars and doing at least three individual consultations per week or month by a specific date.

Your goals must be **SMART:**

Specific

Measurable

Attainable

Realistic

Timed

An important feature of goals is that you must know when you have accomplished them. "I'm trying to get some speaking engagements with associations" is not a goal. "I will speak at five association meetings by December 31 this year" *is* a goal. Committing to a goal and reaching that goal by a certain date, no matter what happens, proves to yourself that you can be a powerful producer of results.

To help you identify your goals, try "mapping out" your business. This exercise is like taking an aerial snapshot; seeing your goals as a whole with many parts. When we begin the goal-setting process, we tend to bog down in the details and fail to see how the

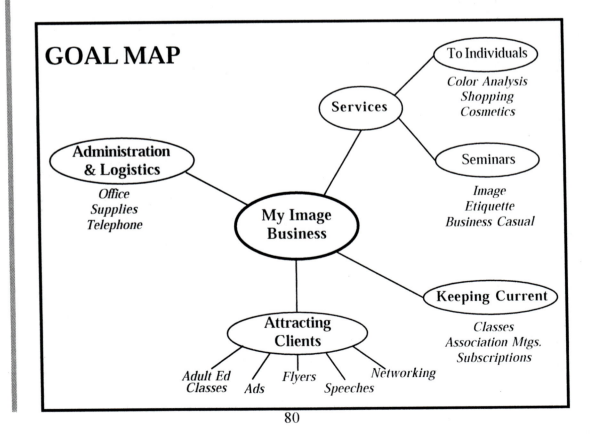

various parts connect to and affect each other. When viewed as a map, you may appreciate better the interconnections and the opportunities for cross-selling. For example, you may offer image training to corporate clients in addition to consulting with individuals. To the corporate client, you may offer seminar programs where you come in once, include a clothing demonstration, and leave the participants with a workbook in which to write their individual goals for their image. The objective is that they will take your teaching, embody it, and make positive changes in their lives. If you are very effective, they will naturally go back to the workplace and teach others what they have just learned. Sharing your information with others may lead to individual clients for you.

On the other hand, you may engage your individual clients in a long-term process and really come to know them well. Do they work for companies and could they make the introduction for you into the training department? Your individual clients may love regular newsletters on fashion trends and business dress. You might even suggest that they could use parts of it for their company's internal bulletin. As a contributor to their in-house newsletter, you will have credibility and name recognition. Now no longer a cold lead, the company's human resource professional will be more willing to hear about your other services and seminars. The newsletter could also be sent direct to forty other targeted companies and become the basis of your spring marketing campaign.

The point here is to look at your business as a whole and discover the various channels that provide you business. Wherever there are people, referrals and cross-pollination of leads can result. Your goals will naturally emerge from your marketing plan on the one hand and your personal and professional needs on the other.

Creating Interim Goals

From your birds-eye view, you can see that even one goal may have many parts to it. Decide on your ultimate goal and then work backwards to fill out the interim goals that make the first one possible. For example, one major marketing goal could be to add five new organizational clients by May 31. Your steps—working backward—leading to that goal could be:

5. Cold call 20 women's and men's civic groups and associations by April 30 and set appointments with them.

4. Cold call the decision-maker in each of your target companies: 10 per week by March 31 and set appointments.

3. Send out newsletter, brochure, and cover letter to 40 targeted companies and 20 associations and civic groups by March 5.

2. Write and format newsletter by February 1.

1. Build a database of 40 targeted corporate clients and 20 civic groups and associations by January 16.

By working backwards, some people can more easily see the steps needed to achieve their primary goal.

Personal Growth Goals and Strategies

If your goals are in the personal growth category, write out the pathway to arrive at each one. These strategies or broad methods of fulfilling your goals should be based on a plan for the whole project to launch your business. Consider the following examples:

- You want to tap into the male market but lack the skills. Some useful strategies at this point would be to gain some formal education, align with a sales representative in the store you want to frequent, read all the best literature on menswear and talk to knowledgeable people in the menswear business everywhere: custom shirt shops, menswear stores, custom clothiers, and tailors. Then practice with a few male clients free of charge to gain experience.

- Your goal is to deliver color analysis services by August of this year. Your strategy is to become trained in these skills and to purchase your diagnostic tools.

- Your goal is to provide seminars on business casual dress and professional image by the end of this year. Your strategy may include developing a workbook, buying or creating visuals to teach the topics, and sending out a direct mail piece to human resource professionals. This could also be the start of your marketing plan.

What roadblocks or challenges do you foresee that will inhibit you from accomplishing those goals? How will you overcome each one in turn? The answers to these questions might turn into strategies for you to set in place. Each of us has our own success inhibitors, such as procrastination, lack of cash flow control, or a weak commitment to follow through. Sometimes a little voice seems to whisper in our ears and say, "Are you kidding? There's no way you can do that!" The wisest course is to be truthful and acknowledge your natural roadblocks: either learn to overcome them, make friends with them, or hire a coach to help you manage life with them. In business, the old adage "the truth will set you free" could not be more appropriate. We can only overcome a problem we know exists. The ones we either do not acknowledge or pretend are not there will repeatedly present themselves before us as invisible brick walls and constant opportunities to learn life's lessons.

Action Plan

For each of your strategies, write out a specific to-do list and plot this into your day timer as part of your daily actions. Be specific. Consider the following elements of a specific action plan. Do your daily strategies sound like this?

Monday: Attend Chamber of Commerce networking meeting. Make five contacts.

Tuesday: Call Chamber of Commerce contacts about a business casual program.

Wednesday: Write a letter of introduction to send to human resource managers.

Thursday: Add new contact names to database.

Friday: Phone five clients to follow up on their last consultations. Ask each client for two other referrals and an introduction.

Developing deadlines and timelines for yourself is an important step in setting and meeting goals. Your power lies in your ability to achieve results consistently. Velocity itself creates momentum. Things that drag on lose their impetus. Sometimes even the inspiration that motivated you in the first place is diluted, or evaporates completely. Keeping yourself on track is an effective method of motivation. You will discover that holding your vision in the forefront at all times as an incentive will help you (a) keep your focus, (b) make decisions that support you in expressing your vision, and (c) choose strategies that move you toward your goals.

Worksheet

My Vision is:

_____
_____
_____
_____
_____
_____
_____
_____
_____
_____
_____
_____

My business looks like this (do a mind map of your business, putting yourself at the center or heart with arms reaching out to all the areas that you envision yourself working towards):

My business mind map:

Worksheet

Identify three areas of your business (i.e., services, skills development, marketing, supplies, administration). For each area, list five goals you intend to accomplish and a by-when date.

_____ by when: _____

1. _____
2. _____
3. _____
4. _____
5. _____

_____ by when: _____

1. _____
2. _____
3. _____
4. _____
5. _____

_____ by when: _____

1. _____
2. _____
3. _____
4. _____
5. _____

CHAPTER EIGHT

Finding the Training and Experience You Need

Now that you have written your vision statement, identified some of your goals, and maybe even mapped out some strategies for developing your business, it is now time to fuel the engine that will put your dreams and goals into motion. Education, knowledge, and confidence will help you launch your practice and maintain a successful business foothold as an entrepreneurial image consultant. To accomplish this goal, you will need to write out specific action steps, as we discussed in the last chapter. Part of your plan should be to gain the skills necessary to develop, operate, and grow your image consulting business.

Go back and look at the results of your assessment profiles in chapter 2, and compare the results with your goals and dreams. Identify the skills you will need in order to take you to the next level.

Training and Education Options

Make a list of what you need from a business and marketing standpoint to start your business. Using a highlighter, mark your list of "absolutes," or must-have, skills. Now you can look at the training resources, do your research, and make choices based upon your needs.

"Anyone who stops learning is old, whether at twenty or eighty. Anyone who keeps learning stays young. The greatest thing in life is to keep your mind young."
—Henry Ford

For example, you must have business cards, letterhead, and some kind of brochure. Do you have the skills to design and produce these items? If not, a few training options are open to you. You could attend adult education classes in graphic design and business writing to obtain these skills. You could also have a logo designed by a graphic artist and a brochure developed by someone who has excellent business writing skills. Perhaps you could barter for these services or use design or writing students who would be glad to have some real-life experience. Either way, you will undoubtedly have a hand in the creation and learn from the experience.

How are your marketing and self-promotion skills? If you are terrified about picking up the phone, you might benefit from some marketing and sales courses. You can find such instruction in adult and continuing education institutes, local community colleges, and day-long private classes such as Skill Path that visit different areas from time to time. Trade and professional associations like ASTD (The American Society of Training and Development) and your local Chamber of Commerce often have current information about such seminars. AICI (the Association of Image Consultants International) puts on a convention every year and always includes sessions on sales and marketing. Be sure to join AICI and attend the convention. The Small Business Administration (SBA) in your area also has information on many different types of business

Questions to Ask Training Companies:

• What are the learning outcomes? What can I expect to learn in very specific terms?

• What is the cost and duration of the program? Days, hours?

• What is included? Materials? Meals?

• What extra materials are recommended for purchase?

• What teaching methods are used? Interactive, lecture, demonstration? How much practical application is built into the program?

• What is the teaching environment? Classroom, in hotel, consulting space?

• What is the class size? How many per session and why?

• What prerequisites do you need to comply with?

• What experience, credentials, and expertise do the trainers have? How long have they been training and/or been in the image business?

• What will be the additional travel costs?

• Are there any discounts or payment plans?

• What follow-up coaching support and communications are available? Are they included or for an extra fee?

• Is the location of the training a factor?

• Does the program offer a certificate and CEUs?

• Can I speak to any graduates? What do others say about them?

• Are the marketing materials up to the standard or beyond that of my target market?

• How would you rate the level of professionalism? How quickly does the company respond to your communications?

• Do they offer internships? Under what terms, conditions, and expections?

Next, take a look at your technical image needs. If, for example, you intend to offer color and closet analysis and personal shopping, and you have little or no training or experience here, then you should look for training companies that offer foundation courses. These courses include topics such as color theory, wardrobe planning, principles of fit and garment construction, menswear, fabric, and basic design principles.

On the other hand, if your business focus is offering training programs on image, business protocol, and communication skills to corporate clients, then you will need to have skills and credentials in corporate image, verbal and nonverbal communication, and business etiquette. You will also need to know how to facilitate and develop a seminar or workshop. This type of training provides guidelines for organizing your material and educational methods in order to teach effectively. A few image training companies specialize in seminar development, training skills, and educational methods. (See appendix)

How are your desktop publishing skills? Always remember that you are an image company, and your materials need to represent your profession. You may need excellent printed materials and workbooks to accompany a corporate seminar. Will you learn desktop publishing skills, or will you hire an expert in graphics and computer design to help you in this area? Some image training companies include a package of diagnostic tools and presentation materials such as slides, transparencies, CD-ROMs, PowerPoint presentations, and workbooks. If you want to begin working immediately, these types of professional start-up materials will be extremely useful.

Department Store Programs

If you work in-store, many department stores will train you in sales and image-related skills. These training programs are generally designed for the store's entry-level associates, and may fall under the umbrella of sales and merchandising. As a sales associate, you are more likely to receive training in fashion coordination, product knowledge, and sales. You will be less likely to learn image consulting skills such as body and line analysis.

fashion personalities, or lifestyle assessment to understand a client's needs. Remember that the purpose of the store personnel and personal shopper is to sell merchandise. However, the overriding benefit of working in-store is the experience with clients: communicating with the customer, fitting clothes to a variety of body types, and adapting current fashion to the client's needs. Through this experience and your other education (books, classes, and training programs), you will begin to develop a successful consulting style of your own.

If you already have a clientele, or "book" of clients, you may be eligible to work in the personal shopping office of the better department stores. As an experienced personal shopper, you will perform the same image consulting assignments as private personal shoppers. They keep in communication with an active client list, follow up on their clients' working wardrobe needs, and dress them for special events. They even suggest gifts for the holidays. The in-house personal shoppers also notify their clients of upcoming sales, bonus points, and special in-store events such as trunk shows or fashion shows. In this capacity you would be able to utilize and refine many of your fashion and image consulting skills. Most important of all, you will learn communication skills, wardrobe planning, coordination, and the art of selling clothing to a client. Stores with this type of personal shopping service available are Marshall Fields, Nordstrom, Macy's, and some of the other Federated stores.

Internships

You may be fortunate to live within reasonable proximity to a seasoned consultant with the expertise and experience that you seek. If so, you could present yourself as an intern. Some large department stores will provide the same service, especially to fashion schools with which they have developed a long-term relationship. Paying and non-paying internship positions may be available, each of which is independently arranged. Be prepared to interview for this opportunity as if it were a paying position, and also prepare to be flexible. This interview is an opportunity for the veteran to see if your contributions are a good fit for her practice. You can also use this opportunity to find out if the consultant has experience you can benefit from.

A successful internship is a work/learning exchange. You may wonder why you should work for someone else for free when you can work for yourself. As an intern, you work in order to learn the ropes. Eventually you will learn everything you need to know by being in your own business. But at the beginning, you can save yourself from costly mistakes and unpleasant surprises by apprenticing with a seasoned professional or working in a store. The difference is in the type and speed of training. Classroom learning and textbooks give you a foundation of skills and knowledge. Through interning, you will learn quickly from your experience through exposure and the experience of your mentor or sponsor.

In a successful internship you can become exposed to behind-the-scenes consulting approaches, organizational systems, time management, and marketing styles. By assisting and observing your mentor, you will rapidly discover your own strengths and challenges. You may be pushed beyond your comfort zone to perform certain tasks, and you will soon recognize the difference between "Big Hats" and "Little Hats." A "Hat" in this context means a job or function that you perform as an entrepreneur. Some of these functions, or hats, comprise a large part of your consulting activities and can be thought of as BIG HATS. These come naturally to you, and you perform them well. However, your own natural talents take you only so far in an entrepreneurial business. Other jobs you may have to do as part of running a business, such as bookkeeping, data entry or desktop publishing, may not come naturally. In an image consulting business, these can be considered LITTLE HATS. You may discover a variety of hats that, in the long run, can be worn much more effectively by delegating them to someone else.

Use the interview with a potential mentor or employer to your own advantage as well. Take this opportunity to clarify information, perhaps even information you feel uncomfortable asking about. Here are some questions to ask:

- Does the sponsor or consultant-employer have experience in areas you do not? What are those areas?
- What is the time commitment? Number of hours per session, days per week, and the duration of the internship (number of months)? *A word of advice: the longer your sessions and more frequent your attendance, the more realistic an exposure you can expect and the faster your learning process will be.*

- Is the sponsor open to communicate with you freely? Are you compatible?
- What tasks will you be performing as your contribution to the sponsor's business?
- What business functions will you be observing and in what capacity: observation or actively participating?
- What is included or available? (You need to know the boundaries or anything that may be off-limits to you.)
- Will you receive college credit and how is that arranged?
- Will there be a report or review every month, and how will your tutor be appraised of your progress?
- If you have ideas, when is an appropriate time to suggest them?
- Will you have to do special projects, administrative work, image consulting, and help with seminars?

Learning on Your Own

Much published information that can aid your technical and business skills development is readily available. You should be scouring bookstores and online publishing resources for anything and everything that will provide you with information and techniques. Read about your target market, the services you will be offering, the profession itself, and topics of interest to your target market. The resource section of this book lists numerous other books, magazines, and trade publications as examples. You do not need to read everything, but do select specific titles and publications that are a must for you. For example, if you are targeting mothers going back to work, you may want to read *Working Mother* magazine. If you are working with a niche market like the plus-size woman, *Mode* magazine is excellent. Fashion magazines give information about upcoming trends. Lifestyle magazines discuss how people of a particular lifestyle live their lives. If you are working with actors, musicians, and other performers, you should read their respective trade newspapers. The two primary image industry publications are *Image Update* (quarterly) by AICI, which comes with membership to the association, and *Image Networker*, which is a trade newspaper available by subscription. If you are working with corporate clients and offering professional development training, you may find *Training and Development* magazine useful. Also, look for other publications from the American Society for Training and Development (ASTD).

Hiring a Coach

In the last few years, coaching has become a popular and fashionable career in itself. Entrepreneurs and corporate executives have found a distinct advantage in partnering with an external business expert to help them reach their goals. The International Coach Federation has written guidelines and policies that helped set the scene for the coaching industry to flourish as a professional discipline.

A coach is someone who has expertise and experience in an area in which you are seeking mastery. You would usually hire a coach for three or four sessions per month, each session lasting one-half to one hour at a time. The coach acts as an advisor, confidant, teacher, and manager to keep your goals on track. The coaching may take place face-to-face, online, by telephone, or through a combination of all three. Just as with an internship, a coach will set up rules, boundaries, and expectations. If your coach is going to spend time giving you pearls of wisdom, you need to respect the professionally structured agreement. You want a coach who pushes you beyond your limits, and who helps you to keep your word and maintain your integrity. You will be encouraged to move out of your comfort zone.

Coaches are trained to be honest, frank, and skilled communicators. To make the coaching relationship a success, you must also be "coachable;" that is, willing to listen and be open to the work assigned. The relationship requires that you allow yourself to be vulnerable, to enhance your personal growth and business development. A coach can give you invaluable feedback and wisdom, and is committed to your success.

You may receive support and any of the following benefits from a worthwhile coach:

- Life balance
- Abundance and financial freedom
- Higher levels of mastery in current areas of operation
- Personal and professional leadership skills
- Communication skills

- Tips on strategic planning and tactics
- Role-playing practice
- A problem-solving forum
- Focus and goal setting
- Shortcuts
- Business and networking leads
- Tips on dealing with difficult situations
- Self-awareness, values, and needs
- Personal and professional vision and mission
- Clarification of your business focus and purpose
- Self-promotion statement
- Marketing and sales strategies
- Practices and procedures to fulfill goals
- Behavior modification

If you desire a professional coach, there is an official association available that provides lists of people in your area. Contact the International Coach Federation at 888-423-3131, or visit their Web site at *http://www.coachfederation.org*. You may also be able to obtain a coach through trade or professional associations, the Yellow Pages, or by contacting consultants and counselors who provide coaching services.

Mentors

Different than a coach, a mentor is a trusted advisor: someone you admire and want to emulate, and who is willing to be your advisor on a less formal basis than a coach. He or she does not typically provide a structured work environment, such as weekly calls and homework assignments, but is someone to whom you can turn for advice on professional or personal problems. This relationship may include fees, but more often the advice is given free.

Tips for Finding Mentors, Coaches, and Internship Situations

If you belong to a professional association or trade group, you will be able to meet potential mentors and demonstrate to them your interest in learning and your capabilities. Demonstrate your commitment by serving on a committee, volunteering your services, and most importantly, asking for support. You may find potential mentors and coaches among previous employers, colleagues, your church or religious group, professionals you admire, wise relatives and friends, or trade associations. Be prepared to invest time in cultivating the relationship. Whether a mentorship or internship, you are asking to be privy to inside information from a veteran--and potential competitor. You must earn their trust.

Questions and Answers about Coaching

by Ruth Zanes (Inspired by Thomas Leonard)

Rlzcoach@aol.com, 678-566-8105

What Is Coaching?

Coaching is a profession that has synthesized the best from transformational philosophies, psychology, business, finance, and personal growth theories to benefit individuals who want to be supported and empowered in reaching personal, business, and career goals.

Why Does Coaching Work?

Coaching works because of three unique features:

Synergy. Client and coach become a team, focusing on the client's goals and needs and accomplishing more than the client would alone.

Structure. With a coach, a client is encouraged and supported to take more actions, think bigger, and get the job done, thanks to the accountability that the coach provides.

Expertise. The coach knows how to help people make more money, make better decisions, set the best goals, and restructure their career, business, professional, and personal lives for maximum productivity and satisfaction. The coach will also have insights into situations and personal barriers that historically have stood in the way of goal achievement.

Who Works with a Coach?

Coaching clients are people from all walks of life who are interested in personal and professional growth and/or have specific goals or situations they want to handle. Coaching clients are typically people who are already successful and seek new challenges or are seeking clarity of purpose and new directions. Clients include entrepreneurs, business owners, corporate executives, managers, professionals, retirees, parents, and people facing family crises. Typical projects and issues include career transition, start-up businesses, business expansion, personal and business financial success, increasing productivity and effectiveness, dealing with health crises, creating balanced lifestyles, enhancing personal and business relationships, etc.

How Does Coaching Happen?

Coaching is delivered during regular, weekly sessions by telephone and/or occasionally in person three times or four times a month. Clients bring an agenda of what they want to work on to each coaching session. The coach helps them solve problems and make the most of opportunities. When the client is missing a principle, distinction, or insight, the coach presents a new perspective so the client can see the situation clearer and from a different point of view. When a client is taking on a large goal, the coach helps to design the project and provide the support and structure needed to make sure it gets done. Coaches bring out the client's best by offering their insights, expecting a lot, helping to strategize, pointing out options, and celebrating the victories.

What Should I Look for in a Coach?

The right coach brings out your best, consistently. To accomplish this, the coach you select should pass the following four criteria:

1. Does this coach have appropriate training in coaching skills, life experience, and recognition from other coaches as a basic foundation?
2. Does this coach have a track record of helping someone like me to accomplish goals similar to mine?
3. Will this coach keep up with—and ahead—of me as I grow?
4. Do I feel good and motivated to act when I am with this coach? Do I feel the chemistry is right between us?

How Much Do Coaches Cost?

The fees for coaching range from $250 to $1500 per month, depending on the number of sessions and frequency of sessions. Corporate programs, workshops, and seminars are priced on a custom basis.

How Do I Start Working with a Coach?

Coaching is not something that is sold; you buy it because *you* want it and you or your company wants to invest in you. Most coaches begin with a preliminary meeting (by phone or face-to-face) with the client to get to know one another. The coach wants to hear about the client's goals, problems, and needs. The client wants to be comfortable with the coach. During this meeting, both parties design a list of goals and a game plan to reach these goals. Prior to this meeting, the client will have received a welcome package that contains a series of assessment materials and essay-type questions to answer. All are designed to maximize the value of the work.

How Long Do I Work with a Coach?

Most coaches ask for a minimum three-month commitment, but only if both the client and coach enjoy the process. After that the length of time depends on what the client's needs are. Some clients work with their coach for years, and they intend to include coaching as an ongoing part of their life. In many cases, clients come back periodically as they encounter new situations or face new projects and goals. Clients and coach generally know when the appropriate time comes to end the coaching agreement.

What If I Feel That I Am Not Getting the Results I Expected?

You must be willing to communicate your feelings and tell the truth to the coach, who will be open with you as well. Your coach should have boundless love, compassion, strength, and understanding for whatever you are feeling; also, if the client does not begin to experience success, I suggest that they find another coach.

What Is the Difference between Coaching and Therapy?

Coaching is goal-driven, fast-paced, and action-based. Coaching works from the premise that the client is already whole, competent, and strong. Coaching produces paradigm shifts. In contrast, therapy is based on discovering the why of behavior. Therapy focuses on the gradual healing of hurts experienced in the past. The coach is not a therapist. However, coaches frequently do report shifts in behavior, the disappearance of counterproductive, repetitive behavior patterns, and inner peace and satisfaction. The coach will help the client face up to self-generated barriers, as well as increase understanding and appreciation of themselves and others in their lives. If the coach feels that the client would benefit from therapy, that recommendation will be made. Some clients work with a coach and a therapist at the same time.

What If I Don't Know What I Want and Have No Goals?

Many clients come to coaching with this complaint. My expertise is in allowing people to discover their purpose, and to create a vision and mission. Personal and business goals naturally evolve once a person embraces his or her purpose and dreams.

What If I Know That I Can Never Achieve My Goals Because of the Practical Realities of Life?

Coaching is about designing a life you love to live and not settling for anything less. In the coaching process, you can discover that you can have what you want and you can find out how to get it.

CHAPTER NINE

Promoting Your Business

Networking

Attracting business to you is part of the art of being an image consultant. If people like the way you look, they will want to dress like you. You become one of your own best marketing tools every time you appear in public. You are a walking, talking advertisement for your own service. If you consistently show up at networking events looking the part and speaking persuasively about your services, people will gradually associate your name with your positive image and you will develop a reputation as a consultant. Attend association meetings and business "after-hours" events where you have the opportunity to introduce yourself to potential clients and contacts and exchange business cards. Everyone has the potential to be a client or to introduce you to another valuable lead. You never know where your business will come from.

"When you give other people what they need, they will give you what you want."
—Anne Boe
from Networking Success

Leads Clubs

A leads club is an effective way to get the referral process going when you first start your business. A leads club usually has twenty to thirty members, each with a different specialty, who meet at breakfast, lunch, or after work. Most networking clubs work with a similar structure. Everyone is given 30 seconds at the beginning and end of the meeting to announce who they are and what services or products they provide. On a rotating basis each person is given about ten minutes to make a presentation in more depth. To start business coming to you, giving your fellow members a discount or special rate is a good idea, so that they can try out your services and then start referring you to others.

Personal Referral

Since image is so personal, people like to see you or have heard about you before they buy your services. Marketing yourself through personal referrals is always best. Every time you do a consultation, workshop, or seminar you should leave people with a list of your services or your brochure or business card. Ask people to recommend you to others. Give out free gifts if you have a product. Offer your consultation as part of a raffle and then call all the others who signed up but didn't win.

Speaking Engagements

If you enjoy speaking in public you can use your skills as a marketing tool. Speak everywhere and become known in your community. Look in your phone book for the list of associations, clubs, and civic groups likely to need speakers. They are all looking to fill their rosters, and even if you have to speak for free at first, it is a way of making yourself known in the community. Check out your local Adult Education Programs often sponsored by high schools, libraries, churches, and civic and religious organizations. Invariably, networks such as the Learning Annex, Discovery Center, and continuing education centers at local colleges offer seminar series, and they may be the ideal place for you to develop and hone your presentations.

Writing Articles

Your local newspaper is also looking for articles and columns. You could establish yourself as the expert by producing a question-and-answer column every week. You could also offer articles on image-related topics. Even if your articles are not accepted at first, keep trying. You are establishing yourself as a credible resource, and eventually the fashion editor may call you for your advice the next time she needs an image expert. Your name in print lends a lot of credibility to your reputation. Your persistence pays off here because there is usually a lot of competition for newspaper and magazine space. Make sure that you send regular press releases to your local media to keep your name and services on top of their pile of ideas.

Advertising

The personal touch always works best for an image consultant. Save your marketing budget for newsletters, a simple brochure, and personal flyers advertising your workshops and consultations. Advertisements in newspapers and magazines may not be the best value for your money because of the personal nature of image consulting. A free Yellow Pages listing might be useful just to have a presence in your community telephone book. In most telephone directories, you receive a free listing if you have a registered business telephone line. An advertisement where you can mention your services and products will cost you a monthly fee, usually payable with your monthly telephone bill.

Direct Mailing

Mailing brochures, letters of introduction, postcards, and flyers can be costly and usually only serve as awareness tools. At first, direct mail might bring a return of less than 1 percent. This return increases with frequent mailings; marketers often refer to "the six touch," which indicates that people may respond after hearing your name six times. Direct mail is used most effectively when advertising a new product, educational class, or service, which is discounted or offering a one-time special rate. Even then, several mailings might have to be sent. The return on such a marketing piece dramatically increases with the addition of telemarketing. If you can talk to the people who have received your flyer, you stand a better chance of gaining their attention and capturing their interest. Direct mail is most effective to people who know you or have heard about you. Make sure you collect names and addresses after every event you do, to add to your database of warm leads.

Align with Other Experts

If you want to give a workshop or a talk, think about joining forces with another consultant or boutique. Image consulting is a natural adjunct to career consulting, weight loss clinics, hair styling, and public speaking classes. Other specialties that lend themselves to image consulting services are cosmetic surgery and dentistry, day spas, eyeglass clinics, makeup and paramedical services, some therapy and counseling clinics, job and interview preparation, recruiting, and outplacement services.

Cause Marketing

Partner with a charitable cause by offering your professional services; better yet, contribute your time to the production of an event such as a walk, fashion show, or sports tournament. This gives you the privileged opportunity to develop valuable relationships with movers and shakers in your community. You will learn useful lessons in business and organizational practices and the art of dealing with all types of people!

Newsletters

Always a wonderful method of keeping in touch with clients and potential clients, newsletters are more engaging than flyers and advertisements and can be used to inform people about your services in a way that is interesting and attractive. Think also about creating a Web site and adding a newsletter or question-and-answer section to the information about your company. Keeping the newsletter full of information will cause readers to look forward to receiving and reading it. Give them a reason to pass it on to a friend by giving them an incentive. For instance, for each person whose name and contact information they send to you, the referring person receives _____. Fill in the blank with a gift or discounted follow-up service. Remember to send your newsletters to your local media contacts on a regular basis.

Become the Expert

Try to position yourself in front of the media as often as you can. Start by sending your local media (newspapers, magazines, television, and radio) press releases of events you participate in, conferences you have attended, and awards you may have received. Your community service activities may come in handy here. Send them tip sheets as well. Everyone likes tips, as they are informational and can serve to fill space when needed. Statistics are also very much in demand to support the credibility of your work as an image consultant in the marketplace. Talk radio can also have value. Listeners loyally tune in to their favorite talk shows and often do so with pen and paper in hand. Here also, be prepared to provide tips and useful information to the viewers and listeners. Learn to speak in sound bites. You could also prerecord your tips in 30- to 60-second segments and send them to your local talk show host. A radio audience is a very wide market. Make sure all your tips are of interest to as many market segments as possible.

Technology

Build a client list, and e-mail clients and potential clients with upcoming workshops, tips, and quotes. Give away a small portion of your services for the greater benefit of introducing them to your long-term products and services. For example, you might advertise a TeleClass for free or a small fee on figure challenges and how to overcome them. Participants could share local resources and Web sites for unusual and useful products. Offer a special service for Mother's Day or Valentine's Day. Provide college graduates with a consultation and shopping spree for a set fee, discounted from your normal hourly rate. If you decide to develop a Web site, research your favorite sites and identify why you like them. Ask yourself what entices you to revisit them. The most successful sites are the ones that are easy to bring up on your screen (save time downloading), and which offer tips and information updated on a regular basis. Remember that image consulting is a business of relationships. Find ways to relate to your audience as easily online as you might in person.

Cold Calling

Cold calling is not what it used to be. We no longer bombard a complete stranger with a litany of our services. Rather, we identify needs and problems and solve them through our consultations, services, and products. Instead of calling unknown names on your "hit list" of target clients, do your homework. For the corporate market, research potential companies that typically offer training; learn about their industry needs and some of the issues they may be currently facing. For example, a company's poor reputation might become an image issue. An organization may be experiencing customer service issues

"The more effective you are at selling, the more successful you will be in every area of your life."
—Brian Tracy

due to poor image, weak communications, and low employee morale. If you have met someone briefly at a networking event, call and invite the person to coffee, lunch, or breakfast to learn more about his situation. You are now in a position to offer your services as a solution. Build a relationship with this person out of which they will consider hiring you to work with their employees. Be someone with integrity. If you request 30 minutes of their time for the first meeting, be certain to manage your presentation to be no more than 15 or 20 minutes long, leaving time for questions. A person's professional time is precious.

Your Marketing Materials

Your marketing materials should represent the image business. They should be on high-quality stationery, with up-to-date graphics, printing, and logo. The colors you use should be consistent with your target market. For example, you would avoid pastels and flowers for a corporate brochure. Hiring a graphic designer to help you through this process is well worth the expense.

On the other hand, don't start with an expensive four-color brochure right at the beginning. In the first months of your business, you will be adjusting to your market, establishing your products and services, and developing a philosophy. Wait at least 8 to 12 months before launching into high printing and marketing costs.

Going Prospecting?

Where do you start and how? How are you going to promote yourself to an individual in a networking situation or to a decision-maker in a company? The operative words here are *planning* and *practicing*.

Each consultant should develop an "elevator statement This is the self-promotional piece you have prepared about your company that will powerfully and expressively describe what you do. In its most succinct form, this statement should not take longer than the ride from the first to the thirtieth floor in an elevator. With the pace of living accelerating by the minute and with the information overload that many of us experience, we no longer have the luxury of time to explain ourselves. Nevertheless we need to create an interest the moment we open our mouths. Use the model discussed at the end of this section to slot in the information you want to get across, either for a 30-second mini-introduction or for a longer networking conversation. With practice, you could even expand this model to fit into your sales presentation and biography.

You should be able to add and subtract various sentences and substitute different examples depending on the person you are talking to. You may want to prepare a few different elevator statements so that, given the opportunity to interest a potential client in your services, you will never be at a loss for words. Each statement should be appropriately crafted to the listener's situation.

Make sure you sound friendly and natural. Nothing is worse than an elevator statement that sounds like a rehearsed monologue. If you are interrupted by your companion, enter into a pleasant dialogue and ask questions. The only time you need it intact might be for your seminar introduction or during a leads club meeting.

Your 30-Second Commercial Should Include the Following Elements:

1. *State your name, title, the name of your company, and a little background.*

2. *Describe the services you offer.* Keep the "laundry list" of your products and services to a minimum. Even if you offer the moon and the stars, people can only remember up to about four topics, so consider your audience and tailor the description to them.

3. *Who are your clients?* Give a short list of your best corporate clients if you are speaking to an organization's director of training and development, sales, or human resources. Everyone tends to remember names and numbers more than descriptive speech. If you can use memorable names and statistics, so much the better.

4. *Describe the benefits of doing business with you.* You could be the only image consultant to offer this or that benefit or service. Also, always give a case study or a verbal "before and after story" that illustrates the benefit of doing business with you. Have a different story for each benefit. You might not always have time to tell the whole story, but have a few anecdotes prepared anyway for your longer sales or networking presentations.

   You must create a "hook" or an attention-grabber. Sometimes a bold claim will do the trick, depending on the audience.

5. *Take the next step.* That might be an exchange of cards or an invitation to call for an appointment. You might send them some information or invite them for coffee, lunch, or breakfast to discuss their needs further. You will need to take the lead here; otherwise you will lose good opportunities.

Examples of the Elevator Statement

Example 1

"Hello, I'm Susan Smith, president of Image International. I have had 10 years experience in sales, fashion trends, and marketing with Macy's, Chanel and Glamour *magazine.*

"We offer image consulting services in color, wardrobe analysis, personal shopping, and business protocol for the discerning executive.

"I can save you at least 90 percent of the time it takes you to shop for yourself, and usually with up to 40 percent savings in cost. My clients are often in career transition. For example, a recent client was offered a $10,000 increase in salary because of his enhanced image.

"May we set up an appointment? Here is my card. Would it be convenient to call you on Tuesday morning?"

Example 2

"Hello, I'm Susan Smith, president of Image International. We provide seminars in business image, non verbal and verbal communication skills, and media presentation.

"I have worked extensively with organizations such as IBM, AT&T, and The American Management Association. We prepared the ABC Tennis Team for their Olympic TV appearances.

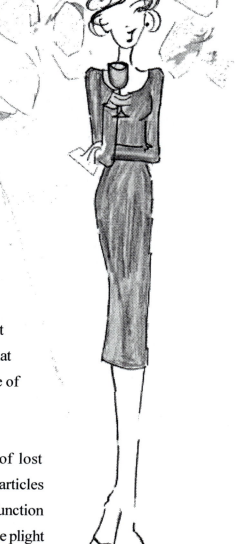

"My background was with CNN and The Bank of America, where I worked in the training departments on media and sales presentations. Sales in the bank increased 35 percent over twelve months as result of our work.

"I would like to fully understand some of the challenges you are facing to see if we could impact them in any way. When would be a convenient time to call you?"

If you have no experience at all, relying on the generalized experience of the image industry is a good approach. AICI is in the middle of a project to archive a collection of articles and statistics that will become an excellent resource for this type of information.

You should keep your ears open for proof of lost productivity as a result of casual dress days and articles proving how business and career success are a function of excellent image. *USA Today* ran an article on the plight of casual business wear and the attempt by management to instigate a return of formal dress codes. ("Companies rethink casual clothes," *USA Today*, 6/27/00.)

Write down success stories of your own and always call your clients and find out what the reaction was to their new image. You can quickly build up a collection of case studies and testimonials of your own.

Information can be deftly incorporated into your statement and will help you sound knowledgeable and experienced. Assuming you have established a rapport with someone at a networking meeting, you can ask him for another, more specific fact-finding meeting when your job would be to see if your services suit his set of challenges.

Example 3

"Hello, I'm Susan Smith, president of Image International. We work with organizations and individuals to improve visual, verbal and nonverbal communication, business protocol, and etiquette.

"Companies are finding that the casual-day trend has had a negative effect on productivity. In a recent poll 1,000 companies were surveyed. Nearly 50 percent cited an increase in absenteeism and tardiness; 30 percent reported an increase in flirtatious behavior after instituting a casual dress policy.

"We have workshops and coaching on appropriate business casual dress specifically for your industry. Here is a brochure outlining our services. I would be interested in your feedback. May we have coffee before our next association meeting and I could find out what's going on?"

WHO DO YOU KNOW?

Jog your memory by thinking of all the people you know ...

AT:

- ☐ your place of business?
- ☐ your doctor's office?
- ☐ your health club?
- ☐ nail/beauty salon?
- ☐ dry cleaners?
- ☐ hospital?
- ☐ your children's school?
- ☐ lawyer's office?
- ☐ florist?
- ☐ your bank?
- ☐ restaurants?
- ☐ _____
- ☐ _____

WHERE YOU BUY:

- ☐ groceries?
- ☐ shoes & clothes?
- ☐ eye glasses?
- ☐ jewelry?
- ☐ furniture? antiques?
- ☐ garden supplies?
- ☐ hardware?
- ☐ greeting cards/gifts?
- ☐ baked goods?
- ☐ arts & craft supplies?
- ☐ books?
- ☐ _____
- ☐ _____

THROUGH YOUR :

- ☐ volunteer work?
- ☐ sports activities?
- ☐ social activities?
- ☐ other affiliations?
- ☐ husband/wife?
- ☐ children?
- ☐ friends & neighbors?
- ☐ relatives?
- ☐ schools, seminars & classes?
- ☐ travels?
- ☐ former employment
- ☐ _____
- ☐ _____

WHO:

- ☐ sells real estate?
- ☐ manages rental properties?
- ☐ sells stocks/bonds?
- ☐ provides catering?
- ☐ owns a business?
- ☐ sells home products?

- ☐ interior decorator?
- ☐ sells office supplies?
- ☐ sells office machines?
- ☐ a career counselor?
- ☐ shrink?
- ☐ sells cosmetics?

- ☐ city, state or federal government worker?
- ☐ works for newspaper, TV/radio?
- ☐ teacher, speaker, lecturer?

My 30-Second Commercial Worksheet

Who am I?

_____
_____
_____
_____
_____
_____
_____

What do I offer?

_____
_____
_____
_____
_____
_____
_____

What are the benefits of doing business with me?

_____
_____
_____
_____
_____
_____
_____

What is my next action?

_____
_____
_____
_____
_____
_____
_____

Your Business Promotion Options

Getting business to come to you takes active participation. You must approach business proactively by having a budget and planning your short and long-term goals, and then take the necessary action steps. You have to let your clients know you and your products and services exist, so they can find you easily. Look at the following list and identify the vehicles for you:

Promotion Vehicles	I can do now	I need to learn	Not for me
Networking			
Leads clubs			
Personal referrals			
Speaking engagements			
Adult education classes			
Writing articles			
Advertising			
Yellow pages			
Direct mail			
Partnering with others			
"Cause marketing"			
Community service			
Newsletters			
Media interviews			
Websites			
E-mailings			
Teleclasses			
Cold calls, breakfast/lunches			
Other			
Other			

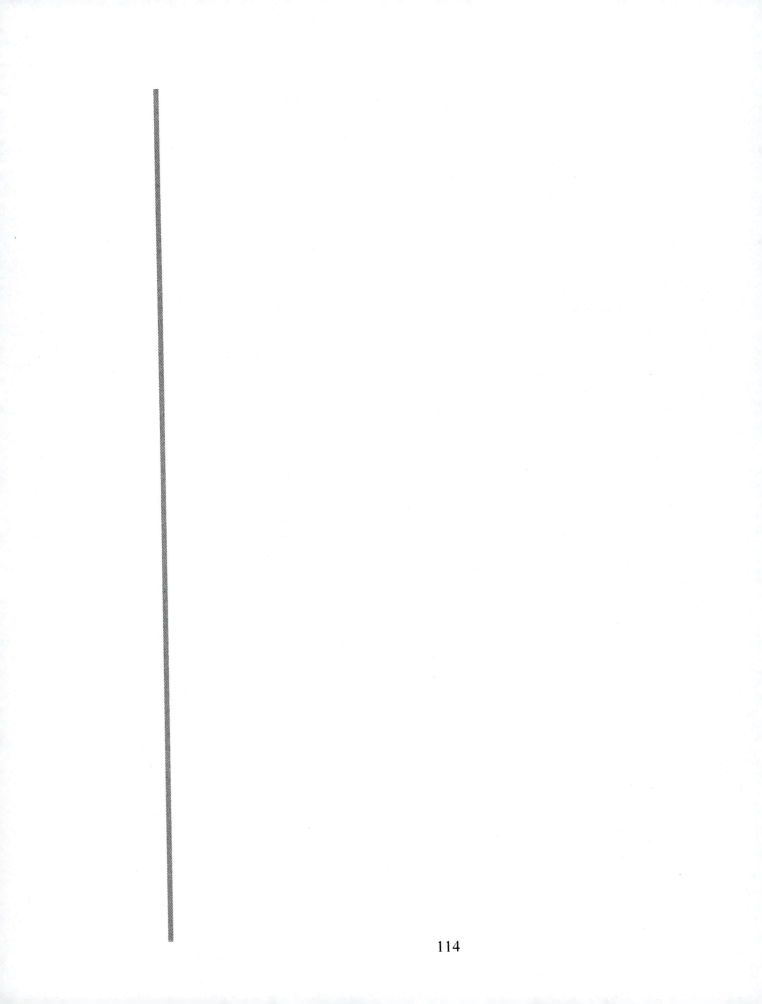

CHAPTER TEN

Making and Keeping Your Money

Let's say that you have some training under your belt, your cards and stationery are printed, you have begun a successful marketing campaign, and paying clients are trickling in. Isn't that great? Yes—if the money you make becomes profit. In a small business, profit means that some money is left over after your expenses are paid.

After many years of training and coaching image consultants, we know several who started to make money but were unable to keep it. No one came in in the middle of the night to take the money away; rather, the cash flow demons took the upper hand.

Go back to the results of your Business Skills self-assessment in chapter 2. If you know you are weak or have no experience in cash flow management, accounting, bookkeeping, or business planning, then pay close attention to this chapter. So many consultants enter this profession with wonderful skills, talents, and a passionate desire to help people through image and communications services; yet not everyone succeeds in keeping their hard-earned money. If you are not making money, you don't have a career—you have a lovely, expensive hobby. If you bought this book, chances are you're interested in making money, too.

Make Friends With and Understand Cash Flow

Cash flow management is a consultant's biggest challenge. The quicker you make friends with it, the sooner you will have money in your bank account. Having ample cash flow means having money available when the bills come in. When you were a salaried employee, you received a set dollar amount each week or month. You were able to plan

"Plan ahead: It wasn't raining when Noah built the ark."
—Richard Cushing

ahead, budget your expenses, and take care of your personal needs. You knew, for example, whether you could afford a vacation each year. On the other hand, as an entrepreneur you are paid for your billable time. Billable time is only time spent delivering services or selling products. You will be performing dozens of other actions to prepare for your consultations—none of which bring in any money. As an entrepreneur, your business is a balance between actual income and expenses. When your actual income does not match your projections and is less than expenses, what happens? What if you had 12 hours of consulting booked with a client whose mother has just taken ill, and the client is relocating to be near her? Or one of your corporate clients just slashed its training budget? Your rent still has to be paid, and you've just paid suppliers for materials ordered for the canceled appointments. You must be prepared for this kind of thing to happen.

If your business is based upon the sale of products and services, you must plan for those clients who may not pay you on time. Take the classic true incident of a clothing designer and a manufacturer whose product was selling like hotcakes…yet both nearly went bankrupt. The retailers increased their orders, but unfortunately did not pay the manufacturer on time for what was already delivered and sometimes even sold. The clothing company could not produce more garments, simply because their operating budget dried up.

We wish we could teach you some guaranteed system to handle your cash flow. Nothing is guaranteed, not even the weekly paycheck from your former employer. But with careful planning and a basic understanding of cash flow, you can learn to manage your business growth and create a successful consulting enterprise, with or without the MBA.

Do Whatever It Takes to Keep the Cash Flowing

Here are some tips for managing your cash flow:

- Plan easily accessible financial options. Know where you can get cash if you need it: alternative income, credit, family loans or other assets.
- Know the minimum amount of money you need each month. What is your bare minimum?

- Start with a cash cushion to fall upon just in case. Have 3–6 months' overhead expenses in cash reserve or in available credit.
- Be proactive. Don't wait for business to wander in through your door. Make it happen through attraction and other forms of marketing.
- Know your costs of doing business—materials, overhead expenses. You need a handle on this information to set appropriate fee rates.
- Keep your overhead very low.
- Put your taxes aside regularly. Don't mess with the IRS.

Businesses whose cash dries up simply go out of business. Unless you are independently wealthy, you will need to be sure of where the money is coming from in your business.

Know Your Breakeven Point

A business plan is important. If you've written one, you will know your breakeven point. If not, you'll need to pay close attention to Chapter 11.

When determining where the money is coming from and going to in your business, you should include the following steps:

List and total all of your investment costs

- Training and skills development
- Marketing materials
- Basic start-up supplies and equipment
- Fees for accountants, coaches, lawyers and other professionals
- Dues to professional associations and organizations
- Marketing and sales costs
- Yellow Pages and other forms of advertising

Find out your hard costs of services

What actual costs do you incur each time you perform a color analysis, a personal shopping session, or corporate training program? This list may include color palettes, written handouts, and travel expenses. This cost is a variable expense: the more clients you have, the more your expenses will be. This amount is proportionate to your volume.

Calculate how much you need personally to sustain your livelihood

Include in this list all your fixed expenses:

- Rent or mortgage
- Car payment
- Insurance
- Telephone and utilities
- Interest on loans

Identify what you will charge for each service, product, or program

What is your fee schedule? How much can or will you bill out in a month? This figure influences your marketing needs. You want to be sure you can fulfill the demand.

Subtraction: The *unfun* part

Subtract your monthly expenses from your monthly revenues. Chart it out for as many months as you need to until you make back your initial investment. You may discover that you will need more money to begin with than you thought. Do not worry: this information enables you to plan, and planning is power that leads to profit.

Where will the money come from?

Here's where your strategies begin to work for you. Remember, the difference between a business and a hobby is that a business makes a profit:

- Don't leave it all to chance! Plan your marketing events and projects on a monthly basis.
- How many lead-generating events will you attend each month?
- Where else do you need to show up in your community to create awareness for your business and acquire clients?
- How many cold calls or warm calls must you make to generate one paying client?
- How many workshops and individual consultations must you do per month to cover costs?
- Where will you acquire updated lists of potential corporate clients?
- How many flyers, brochures, and newsletters will you send out each month to land one corporate client?

For Example:

REVENUES

	Month 1		Month 2	
Income - client services				
Color analysis	3 sessions @ $75	= $225	6 sessions @ $75	= $450
Personal shopping	2 hours @ $100	= $200	4 hours @ $100	= $400
Income - group programs				
Seminars	1 @ $300	= $300	2 @ $300	= $600
Public speaking	1 @ $0	= $0	1 @ $100	= $100
Income - product sales				
Cosmetics	Total sales	= $150	Total sales	= $300
Workbooks	10 @ $10	= $100	20 @ $10	= $200
Total Income / Month		**$975**		**$2050**

EXPENSES

	Month 1		Month 2	
Variable Expenses				
Cost from client services				
Color analysis	3 x $15	= $45	6 x 15	= $90
Personal shopping		= $5		= $10
Cost from group programs				
Seminars				
Public speaking travel		= $5		= $10
Cost from product sales				
Cosmetics @ 50% cost		= $75		= $150
Workbooks sold at program @ $4/ea.	10 x 4	= $40	20 x 4	= $80
Total Variable Expenses		**$170**		**$340**
Fixed Expenses				
Rent, insurance, utilities, interest on loans, Yellow Pages ads		$1500		$1500
Total Fixed Expenses		**$1500**		**$1500**
TOTAL EXPENSES PER MONTH		**$1670**		**$1840**

As you can see from the previous charts, in the beginning, expenses are commonly greater than income. Do not worry, as long as from month to month the revenues increase. You must continue extending the projections until your revenues are greater than your expenses. At this time you will have reached your breakeven point: the moment when you can start to reimburse yourself for your initial investment.

To handle your cash flow properly, you should evaluate your income and expenses on a regular basis. You will need to manage your expenses so that they do not regularly exceed your revenues. Do not overuse credit cards so that you incur huge debts with astronomical interest rates. Ignorance about your financial situation is business suicide.

Sometimes your business has seasonal ups and downs. A personal shopper, for example, might experience a dip of income in the summer. You must plan to have operating capital saved up or available to you during the slower periods, especially if you are building a business serving the corporate sector. Corporations have their own billing cycles that rarely correspond to your personal bill-paying schedules. The sales cycle—the time it takes from the start to the close of the sale—also varies for different types of image consulting. If you start calling organizations in January, for instance, you may not be booked until March or April at the earliest. To keep the cash flowing, you will need to fill your time with individual business until your seminars start rolling in.

The wisest plan is to plan to have a backup financial reserve. Another word of caution: try not to spend your money as soon as you get it without thinking about what it will bring you in return. One consultant just received a windfall from a client who booked 10 hours of consulting. The consultant rushed out and purchased a brand-new wardrobe for exactly what she just earned. It is very tempting, but rather faulty planning. A wiser plan is to open your own business account and deposit all professional fees and revenues into it. If you want to take out a salary, work out the amount minus taxes. An even better precaution is to sign on with a payroll company who, for a very small fee, can work out your income and deductions as you go. They will also file quarterly returns for little or no charge and keep your tax records updated. You will never have to worry that you don't have enough money for taxes if you make the deduction at the source.

"By failing to prepar[e] you are preparing to fail."
—Benjamin Franklin

Setting Your Fees

"What is my time and expertise worth?" is a different question than "What will people pay for my time and services?" If you have never had to put a value on your time, then this question could be a challenge for you. Placing a value on the sale of a product is easier because it is less personal. *The product costs $20 to produce and I want to earn $20 from the sale; therefore I will charge the customer $40.* You can start by looking at your hourly rate, at the going rate for your market, at your experience, and even at what you want to earn in a week or month. A serious reflective moment is useful here, as you want to separate your self-worth from the professional value you provide to your clientele. You will notice that the two are rarely the same. The value you put on your head is often much lower!

A range of external components can also set your fees. Your geographic region, for instance, will determine the range of prices you can charge for individual consultations. In a small rural town you will not be able to charge as much as in New York or San Francisco. Indeed, an image consulting business in the fashionable metropolitan cities will charge more for all services such as color analysis, seminars, fashion shows, and workshops. In rural areas where the costs of living and doing business are lower, your service charges will also be lower. Compare your prices to those of interior design consultants in your area and you will be able to gauge yourself in that range. The Financial Matrix in chapter 5 can give you a benchmark.

You could also research the costs of haircuts and chemical services in a typical hair salon that your clients might frequent. For example, if your clients are accustomed to paying $150 for a hair color treatment, then they will be comfortable spending a similar amount for an image consultation. Remember that clients who regularly have their hair colored usually have this in their budget to spend every four to six weeks. A client paying $50 every eight weeks for a color treatment will be very unlikely to spend more than $50 to $75 for an image-related service. This formula helps you work out the range of prices the client will tolerate in your particular target market. You can also use these comparisons in your sales presentations.

Your experience also counts enormously. The more experience you have, the more confident you will feel about charging professional prices. Keep in mind that, as a consultant, your experience is cumulative. You can count as part of your experience all the different related jobs you have had. If, for example, you have had five years experience in a retail boutique and four years selling a makeup and skincare line, and you raised a family for six years—during which time you regularly dressed friends and family and are now ready to start an image consulting business—you have 15 years experience. You are not a beginner. Your confidence might need a boost at first, so you could start with lower fees; as soon as you see the difference you are making for your clients, you could raise your rates.

Free Sessions

Many consultants will offer complimentary seminars, presentations, and demonstration clinics. Find out who would value a free session and ascertain what the return on investment would be to you. If your work includes cosmetic sales, it is customary to offer makeup application demonstration sessions to individuals and groups in a house party format. The demonstration shows your target client how to use the product. This invariably leads to product sales. If you work with corporate groups, you may consider offering a free session as a marketing tool to decision-makers who could use your services afterward. Again, part of your marketing strategy should include speaking at association, civic group, and various business networking meetings. These gatherings may offer a small fee or an honorarium, but often they do not. Nevertheless, these unpaid sessions are a great way for you to market your services.

Another way for people to assess your work would be to do a pilot seminar or workshop. In this case, you could present a public seminar on a topic of relevant interest to a specific market, such as a seminar on business casual for human resource professionals. This seminar serves as an audition platform for you. A successful program may lead to in-house training opportunities of much greater financial return than your investment to produce the public seminar.

When you give things away, you want to be clear in your own mind why you are doing so, and what anticipated return you expect. Community service programs for a philanthropic organization will always position you positively in the public eye. For instance, image consulting could fit easily with organizations that help people go from welfare to work. It should be done for the sake of good will, with no expectation of a return. If you expect a return, then you are doing it for the wrong reasons and the public may soon discover this. Your return may be in the form of visibility and even press coverage. All this publicity is useful to support your ongoing marketing efforts. Choose your community service contributions carefully, and make sure they align with your philosophy and vision. Unless you are highly skilled, extreme causes with strong political attachments could become public relations risks. On the other hand, they could also bring you notoriety, especially if you are an image consultant specializing in media image and damage control from scandal or controversy.

Some Common Costs to Be Expected

When providing services and programs to corporate clients you can expect some of the following costs for services and some of the typical initial investments.

Service	Common costs for services	Common investment costs
To deliver seminars and keynotes	• Research time for meetings and needs assessments • Press kit or marketing package • Workbooks or handouts	• Training for general background • Travel to training site • Technology - computer, fax, etc. • Appropriate wardrobe • Corporate image design • Presentation tools - slides, PowerPoint, visual props, dinner-ware for etiquette • Membership dues
To provide coaching	• Assessment tools/ profiles • Written materials • Travel to client	• Initiation fees and training in use of tools such as DiSC® • Travel to training site • Coaching tools such as video
For media training	• Video tapes • Workbook for client & possible design fee • Travel to client - optional	• Training in presentation and media or similar background • Video camera • Audio recording equipment • Subscriptions to publications

When consulting for individuals, you can expect some of the following variable costs for services and other investments based upon your business offerings.

Service	Common cost areas for services	Common investment costs in order to deliver services
Color analysis	• Personal color charts • Written handout materials • Refreshments	• Skills training • Travel to training • Diagnostic tools - drapes, etc.
Personal shopping	• Travel to the stores • Refreshments if you treat your client	• Skills training • Time researching vendor resources
Closet analysis & wardrobe consultations	• Travel to the client • Written log forms	• Skills training • Wardrobe fitting props-pins, tape measure, hem clips
Makeup application	• Cosmetic samples used in application • Tester brushes and applicators • Cleansers and skin care samples • Written forms for demonstration	• Skills training • Licenses • Start up cosmetic inventory • Start up cosmetic supplies for application and mirror
Direct selling or trunk shows	• Refreshments • Telephone	• Initiation fees • Display racks and mirrors

Factor in the following costs for all types of businesses:

- Rent or workplace overhead

- Health insurance (unless it is covered by an existing plan)

- Telephone and Internet access

- Marketing and networking

- Your personal wardrobe, grooming, and personal maintenance

- Dues to professional associations

- Subscriptions to publications

- Accountant and professional fees

- Car payments

Financial Black Holes

Black holes are not just out there in the cosmos—they also exist in many entrepreneurial ventures. One of the biggest money thieves is time: not enough of it, and poor use of it. If you know your time management skills are weak, you would be wise to invest in a time management system and skills training course. Time management is more than having a beautiful agenda, day planner, or electronic calendar like the Palm Pilot series. It is having a system and using it to your best advantage. Time management is also a lifestyle. Parents who manage a household, family, carpools, school activities, PTA, and volunteer committee work know this scenario. As presidents of an international association, we have managed a business, family, and social responsibilities. During that time we learned how to make friends with the time demons, because we certainly could not waste time fighting them. The old adage is true: Give a job to the busiest person you know, and it will get done.

Look for a time management system that works for you. The appendix suggests programs and system options. The two parts to mastering time management are the system itself and knowledge of priority management. The system is the structure that supports your effective and efficient use of time. If you have to search for phone numbers and forms because you do not have a practical place for filing them, you are wasting time. Each minute you spend looking for something (the average time wasted is two hours a day) is non-billable time. Billable time is when the meter is running and your client is paying the bill. If you spend 20 minutes putting together a marketing packet to send to a potential client because you do not have the pieces in an easily reproducible format in your computer, you are wasting time. Do not spend time waiting at the post office or the office supplies store, or daydreaming at the computer. Mail your marketing materials the day the client calls, not when you get around to it. The sooner your marketing materials arrive in the hands of your prospect, the sooner that prospect may be converted into a client.

Time wasting doesn't only occur in the office. It can happen when you research for your clients or preshop for their wardrobes. By preshopping for multiple clients simultaneously, you make better use of your time than by doing one at a time. Keep in mind, also, that social lunches with your friends may be fun, but can also take you off purpose from your work. Schedule lunch dates when they do not take time away from work, or only if they are directly or indirectly related to networking.

The second part of time management is learning to master the art of priorities. You must choose your priorities in your personal and professional life. How much time do you want or need to spend with your family? How much income do you want or need to earn? How much time do you want or need to invest in your educational and business development? How soon do you need results? Each of these answers influences your personal choices, and we emphasize that the answers are different for each entrepreneur. One size does not fit all.

Interruptions are also time-eating demons that draw us into that black hole. Consultants who work from home are victims of interruptions and distractions. The dog needs to be walked, a child asks a question, the plumber comes to fix the sink, and a neighbor needs your help moving a piece of furniture. This list does not include the social telephone interruptions that may be a welcome distraction when you're having a bad day! Some interruptions are completely out of your control; others are indeed manageable. You may have to train people in your life to respect your time as a professional. It may take a bit of reminding, and may feel awkward at first, but after you do this you will be creating an environment of people and systems that support you in achieving your goals. Reminding yourself of your goals, objectives, and mission will help you to keep your focus. Know how to adjust your priorities to changing circumstances.

How you spend your time is determined by your goals and needs. If your desire is to have a quicker return on your investment because your survival depends upon it, then you will need to spend more money and time on your sales and marketing in order to start earning back your investment. This is where your cash flow or budget projection chart will be handy. One game you can make for yourself is to list all of your income areas or profit centers in the left column. Then, make three additional columns to the right—one for each month of the quarter. Use half of each column for the assignments you are scheduled to deliver, and the other half for work for which you expect to be paid. The reason for separating the two is that if you are working for corporate clients, you may have to wait for payment due to invoicing cycles. For this reason, you may choose to pursue a cash-only business practice with individual clients who pay upon delivery of the service, as you do when you go to the doctor's office. Again, your choices are based upon your goals and financial needs.

This is not a complete cash flow chart, as it does not reflect your expenses, but it can be a fun and helpful visual game board that will help you invest your time in income-producing activities. For example, you may wish to highlight each payment you receive with a bright color. The chart also helps you see how many activities you have that support you in meeting your financial goals. Pro bono programs go in the *To deliver* column, yet these activities may bring you paying business in the months to come.

Don't let yourself fall into a black hole. Making money is actually easier than you think, but regaining lost time is impossible.

The Value of Your Financial Advisors

Each businessperson's needs, goals, and priorities are unique to his or her venture. Consulting with an accountant or financial advisor on a regular basis is a smart move. Your personal financial situation will guide your actions. At any given time, you have to decide whether to reinvest your earnings into the business or your own business development, or to keep it in reserve. Sometimes you need to reward all your hard work with a salary. Your financial advisor will also counsel you on the best tax schedules for your situation and your payment schedules. Do not wait until you are in a financial crisis to consult with an advisor; by then it may be too late. Your advisor can guide you toward the most reasonable credit and loan options and help you prepare your records for the bank. Your financial advisor can be your best friend and ally, ready and willing to coach you to business success.

	September		October		November		December	
	To deliver	Receivable	To deliver	Receivable	To deliver	Receivable	To deliver	Receivable
Programs:								
Client Sessions:								
Product Sales:								
Monthly Totals								

CHAPTER ELEVEN

Writing a Proposal and a Business Plan

The Proposal

An organization has asked you and several other consultants to submit a proposal. Ideally, you would call the decision-makers and talk to them about the challenges they are facing. You may be lucky enough to have several in-depth conversations with your potential client, but more often than not, a quick phone call is all that he will have time to give you.

Your proposal, therefore, must demonstrate that you are professional and have experience dealing with the challenges the client faces, and that you understand his industry. Your proposal must provide a succinct, planned approach outlining how you intend to solve his problems and achieve the results he is after. Think of it as a menu. If he has asked for a hamburger, he doesn't necessarily want a fast-food approach or a three-course meal either. Give him the best-prepared, most creative hamburger he has ever eaten, with lots of trimmings!

Following is a format that is useful when writing large proposals in a competitive bid situation. For smaller proposals—or when you know you already have the assignment—you can pull out some of the relevant sections from this format. Use at least one page per section for your proposal, and use a large typeface with bullets and easy-to-read sentences.

Elements of a Proposal

1) The industry situation or background
2) The objectives
3) The needs
4) The program outline or basic content
5) The benefits
6) The timeline
7) The total investment
8) The references

1) The industry situation or background

Give a brief description of the current situation in the industry you are addressing. You would need to demonstrate, for example, that you are aware of

- The history of the industry, if appropriate
- The changes and challenges they face as an industry
- What the competition is doing to overcome those challenges

This section need not be long but must make the reader aware that you have done your research and intend to match your programs and courses to the current situation. People will be much more comfortable with you if they feel that you at least understand their general circumstances. The situation section will also substantiate your case and validate the programs you are recommending.

Example

The marketplace is becoming increasingly international. In order to survive the competition you need to be aware constantly of the critical role that your corporate identity plays in a global arena. Your identity may include many components such as logo, marketing materials, advertisements, physical environment, and location. Yet another important but often overlooked facet of your corporate identity is also the image and behavior of your employees.

In a business context, the impressions formed by clients, employees, and the public are based upon the impact of **visual presentation** (appearance), **verbal communication** (diction, listening, speaking), **nonverbal communication** (body language, business practices, attitude), and **etiquette and protocol** (appropriate behavior and customer sensitivity).

In a service industry such as yours, personnel with a knowledge of professional image skills tend to build relationships more easily and are more comfortable in unexpected situations than personnel who lack such skills. Unclear messages projected by one's professional presence can cause costly distractions to both the client and the employee. These distractions impact communication skills and ultimately can harm your corporate identity, to the benefit of your competitors.

2) The Objectives

Write three to five broad-based objectives that you intend to accomplish, written in an easy-to-read bulleted format. This list of objectives should attract attention and make the reader curious to read further. Beware of exaggerated claims and "being all things to all people," which reduces your credibility and actually makes you sound generic and less focused.

Example

Our objective is to upgrade the level of professionalism in performance and image at ABC Company by

- Presenting essential business protocol guidelines
- Defining and providing tools to develop professional presence

133

- Providing appropriate image standards and a customized dress code manual
- Creating tools for professional wardrobe management and maintenance
- Introducing and implementing proven verbal and nonverbal communication skills and techniques
- Providing short term in-house training services and long-term personal development coaching

3) The Needs

Write out all the client's needs you have heard, using exact terminology if possible. If you have heard problems, wishes, and hopes, translate all those into needs that you can address with your seminars. For example, a hotel human resource manager might mention that he would like one of his front desk personnel to tie her hair back and wear the appropriate shoes. Your translation would be that they need grooming tips, hair styling, and accessorizing appropriate to front desk hotel personnel. They also might need a dress code and ways to implement compliance procedures.

Example

We understand that all trained staff, sales personnel, and management must

- Refine and upgrade their image and professional behavior
- Convey consistently high standards of professional image, even in casual dress
- Adhere to rules of professional conduct, business protocol, and etiquette
- Learn to avoid breaches of confidentiality and inappropriate language
- Learn ways to communicate with unhappy clients and deal with difficult situations

4) The Program Outline and Basic Content of Each Session

Once you have conveyed to the client that you understand the situation he has presented you, you need to show the client an outline of the program that you will offer to his staff. Look at the following example for a sample of one image consulting program that you can offer to corporate clients:

Example

Visual Communication: Appearance, grooming, and polish

Hair and makeup

Accessories

Strategic dressing principles

Wardrobe and image maintenance

Colors, styles, and fabrics for business and business casual wear

Nonverbal Communication: Subtle body language messages

Managing your own body language

Reading other people and interpreting their intentions

Walking, sitting, handshakes, eye contact

Identifying the power of body posture and carriage

Demonstrations, role playing

Etiquette & Protocol

Lunch and dinner table etiquette

Do's and don'ts for entertaining the client

Networking for business development

Social and business conversation

What to say, how to say it, and when

The Program Content

At this stage all you may need to include are the basic topics. If, however, you must go a step further and provide more detail, the most effective approach is to write specifically what the participants will be doing throughout each session in the form of learning outcomes or learning objectives. Each objective should start with an action verb such as "identify," "develop," "write," "compare," "contrast," "list," "explain," or "present." Each of these explanations indicate what the session participant will be able to do after the training you provide. In this way, you can break down the session into easy-to-understand sections, each with its own objective. This method will eliminate confusion and misunderstanding about the content of the class. In addition, your skills as a salesperson, teacher, presenter, or facilitator will improve because your outline is extremely clear for all concerned.

Example

After our training session, participants will gain the skills to:

- Recognize the importance of visual impact and appearance in business.
- Use colors, styles, and fabrics effectively for a versatile business and business casual wardrobe.
- Coordinate a collection of clothes from business to business casual to weekend casual.
- Coordinate outfits using the appropriate accessories.
- Plan a budget to afford the image needed for their current position in today's business environment.
- Develop a core wardrobe and ways to expand it.
- Identify appropriate hairstyles and makeup for business and business casual.
- Distinguish appropriate outfits for a variety of different business occasions.

5) The Benefits of Each Session for Each Group

In presenting your plan to the company's decision maker, you will want to make sure that the benefits of your presentation are clearly understood. Break down the list into company benefits and personal benefits.

Company Benefits

Be careful that you do not exaggerate the benefits beyond the realistic scope of your class.

For example, if you have heard that morale is low, you cannot necessarily claim that morale will go up as a result of your image class. If, however, you have given an appropriate business image seminar, the individuals in the class will know what colors, styles, accessories, and fabrics are appropriate to help them achieve the visual image they need for their current position. They will also be aware that the image will help them gain a promotion. You will have included budget and lifestyle strategies to attain the image they want and tips on how to mix, match, and coordinate outfits. They will have the skills to fulfill their image potential and achieve their very best look.

If employees are proactive in creating their own excellent image and become effective representatives of the company to the public, the company will benefit in another way. The company identity is formed by many components. The appearance of its personnel is an important but often forgotten aspect of that identity.

Example

After this seminar, ABC Company will be able to

- Implement clear personal appearance standards and uphold optimum standards of professionalism.
- Measure continuous sustainable improvement in the quality of services, employee loyalty, and confidence.

Additional benefits to the company will include

- Members of an organization who are able to demonstrate responsibility for their personal image and social impact, and who can establish a strong competitive advantage by solidifying the corporation's identity. A strong corporate identity is essential to attracting and retaining clients, vendors, and talented personnel.
- Managers who can serve as image role models to staff personnel, creating a unified presence in the organization.
- Personnel who have the skills to represent effectively the firm's image to the community.
- A self-managing, self-motivated group of individuals who can create a team spirit that is more likely to work towards common goals.
- Members of a team who expect to take personal responsibility for their communications and behavior to clients, colleagues, and superiors.

Individual Benefits

You'll also want to present the individual benefits people at the company will realize. This list will serve to motivate the individuals themselves to derive as much as they can from your seminar, which is being provided to them at the company's expense.

Example

- Tips and tools for easy and effective wardrobe management and maintenance are provided.
- Awareness of professional standards is raised, increasing the chances of promotion.

- Levels of personal effectiveness are heightened, facilitating your ability to provide customer service.
- Confidence and personal comfort are strengthened in both business and social situations.

Measurements

Clients like measurements of before-and-after results. These statistics can become part of the benefits section of your proposals. When you have tabulated the results from one company, you can use those statistics to help sell your programs to other organizations. From an educational standpoint, class evaluation scores can be collected and compared. From a business standpoint, many components can be measured. For instance, absentee-ism, sales revenues and profit figures, call-back response time, number of errors, and time and money spent or saved are all useful measurements. In addition, anecdotal evidence that people shaved mustaches, cut their hair, upgraded their standards of casual dress, complied with the dress code more often, and used makeup can be simple proof that employees implemented recommendations from your image and business protocol sessions. You can think up as many ways to measure the success of your classes as your creativity allows. In the proposal, you can outline a selection of ways to measure the effectiveness of your program.

6) The Timeline

List all the preparation, research, surveys, precourse interviews, needs assessments, consulting sessions, classes, presentations, and follow-up coaching calls that you recommend. Set these in an ideal timeframe so that your client can see how he can allocate resources such as time, money, and personnel to your program. If this program is to take place over a period of time and with many departments, it will help your client if you divide it into phases that accommodate his budget and calendar. If you know the actual dates, add these too. Following is an example of how to present the phases of your program:

PHASE 1: Organization and Preparation

- Formulation meeting with management team to specify objectives of the program
- Needs assessment completed
- In-depth interviews with 15 of your personnel from five departments
- Strategic program created, developed, critiqued, and refined by management team and consultants
- Dates and programs set on calendar
- Contract sent, signed, and returned

PHASE 2: Development of Materials

- Develop and seek approval of materials such as color charts, workbooks, and handouts
- Set dates for meetings and classes
- Dress code developed, written, and passed by legal department

PHASE 3: Program Implementation

- Visual communication session for Sales Department
- Visual communication session for Managers
- Nonverbal communication session for Sales Department
- Nonverbal communication session for Managers
- Two nonverbal communication sessions with Sales Associates
- Two social etiquette and business protocol sessions for Sales Department
- Two social etiquette and business protocol sessions for Managers
- Two full-day staff programs

PHASE 4: Debriefing and Evaluation

- Tabulate class evaluations
- Compile class comments
- Evaluate results and compare with the results prior to the program

- Debriefing sessions with management team and human resources manager
- Make necessary changes to program
- Discuss future opportunities

7) The Total Investment

After presenting the information your seminars will provide, it is time to discuss the cost to the client. You will need to provide the following information:

- The number of seminars and the fee you are proposing with a minimum and maximum number of participants permitted in each group
- The estimated number of consulting and research hours you are charging for
- Any volume discounts you are offering
- Billing and payment terms. For example, you could request half the fee on signing the contract and half when the sessions are completed, or some companies may be willing to give you the total amount before the first session starts.
- The out-of- pocket expenses such as hotel, coach airfare, meals, and other travel and miscellaneous items to be paid for by the client.

Example

The figures in the following example are only suggested rates. Consultants should use the rate table in chapter 5 to assess their own fees.

15 Needs Assessment Interviews	$500
Six Training Workshops to Sales Associates (5–6 hours each @ $2,000 per workshop)	$12,000
Six Training Workshops to Managers (5-6 hours each @ $2,000 per workshop)	$12,000
Five Staff Member Training Workshops (8 hours each @ $2,500 per workshop)	$20,000
Dress Code Researched, Written and Developed	$1,000
Total Investment	**$45,500**

ADDITIONAL RATE SCHEDULE

Individual coaching per half hour	$50
Additional consulting fees per hour	$100
Additional half-day training (3–4 hours)	$1,500
Additional full-day training (5–8 hours)	$2,500

Coaching sessions are conducted on site, by e-mail, or by phone. Travel, hotel, and appropriate miscellaneous expenses are additional and paid for by the organization. Workbooks, manuals, and materials: $25–40 per person estimated at the time of contract.

A 50% deposit is required to reserve the program dates. There is a 60% cancellation fee for a program cancelled within 30 days of the program date. There is no extra charge for booked programs that are rescheduled within 60 days.

8) The References

When making the presentation to your client, list all the people you would like this client to call. Provide names, titles, company name, e-mail addresses, and phone numbers. Be sure that you have told all your references the name of your client and the specifics of his call. They are usually delighted to speak on your behalf, but they may need to be prompted as to the topic and the approach to take.

The Business Plan

You may have heard that your business plan is an important first step to starting a business. Indeed, a business plan is an essential and professional element if you intend to approach anyone for financial assistance, even if those people are your best friends, a financial partner, or a family member. Designing a business plan is also a critical first step if you intend to engage the services of a business consultant to help you launch your enterprise. If you are going to start or expand your business and need the added discipline of a road map and a foundation for strategic planning, the business plan comes in handy here, too.

The actual process of completing a business plan has untold benefits. You will be forced to organize your thinking and compare the advantages of your services against those of the competition. You are likely to set much more specific goals and realistic timeframes. You will also become much clearer when you are selling your services, and come across with much more confidence.

(NOTE: The guidelines outlined in this chapter are written under the assumption that you will develop your plan with the intention of seeking external funding. If you are writing the plan for any other reason, use only the elements you need.)

Do's and Don'ts of the Business Plan

Do include an executive summary. This two- to three-page section is a succinct, well-written synopsis of the overall business plan. The summary largely determines whether investors will read on. This section should always be written after the rest of the plan is completed. The whole business plan should be no longer than 10 to 20 pages.

Do clarify the main focus of the products or services and your target markets. Many business plans fall short because they are not crystal-clear, and try to be all things to all markets.

Do be mindful of the fact that you are writing a business plan for an image business. It must be on quality paper stock, and easy to read with a well-designed cover and sensible page layouts. Incorrect grammar, spelling mistakes, typos, unprofessional language, poor organization, and illogical flow can knock the reader out from the beginning. Pay a proofreader to review the plan for unacceptable and unprofessional errors, and pass the whole thing by a knowledgeable colleague for critique and professional scrutiny.

Do organize the presentation. Include a title page that lists your company name, address, phone and e-mail information, date, and contact name or the names of the company's principals. Number the pages and create a table of contents. Use spiral binding and plastic or card stock cover.

Don't use nonassertive or marketing/advertising language or trade jargon. Also, vague words such as "perhaps," "try," "might," and "probably" have no punch and denote lack of confidence on the part of the business owner. On the other hand, overexaggerated claims and superlatives are perceived as hyperbole and will be largely discounted.

Don't make claims such as "the best product or service on the market" unless there is substantial evidence to support your claim. Any generalizations and assumptions should be backed up with independent data, research, testimonials, statistics, and case studies wherever possible. Your plan will have much more credibility and will immediately come alive in the minds of the investors if everything is substantiated.

Components of the Business Plan

Components of a Business Plan

I.   Nondisclosure Agreement
II. Executive Summary
III. Main Business Plan

I. Nondisclosure Agreement

If you have a very unusual product or service that has never been implemented before to your knowledge, you will need a nondisclosure agreement. This one-page document states that the information in the plan is proprietary and is not to be shared, copied, disclosed, or in any way used in whole or in part. The agreement is usually signed, dated, and returned to you before you send out the business plan.

II. Executive Summary

An essential part of the plan, the executive summary consists of two to three pages and summarizes the highlights of the plan. The executive summary must be clear and state in no uncertain terms what you are offering and what's in it for the investor.

A. The Facts: When was the Company formed? What is its basic purpose?

B. Goals: Short-term, Long-term

C. **Success Record:** Past performance; Why will your company be different and why have you been successful?

D. **Products and Services:** What are you marketing? What distinguishes it from the competition? Price, quality, speed of service, uniqueness of service? What factors might impede its success?

E. **Market:** How large is your market? What is its recent growth and potential?

F. **Competition:** Who are they? What services do they offer?

G. **The Target Market:** Demographics of target market; approximate size in region or area targeted; recent growth and reasons for growth; projected growth and reasons for growth.

H. **Financial Data:** For what purpose are you requesting financing? To what stage will that carry the company? What is the exit strategy for investors? What are the five-year revenue and income projections?

I. **Management:** Who are the principals? What is their background and experience? What are their strengths?

III. Main Business Plan

A. **The Company:** This section provides a more detailed description of the company's business, vision, goals, and current successes.

1) What business are you in? Describe your business venture in broad terms and then describe each product and service in more detail.

2) What are your company goals? Write out the top 5 to 10 goals in specific, measurable terms. Even customer satisfaction can be measured. A goal

asserting that you want to be the number-one company in your field needs to be broken down into smaller specific goals.

3) What are the factors that make you successful? What do you intend to do to make your company successful? What are the company's past achievements and strengths?

B. **Products and Services:** This section includes a detailed description or illustration of all current products and plans for future products. Indicate what distinguishes you from the competition. Include any proprietary, unique, or brand names.

1) What patents, trademarks, or copyrights do your products and services have? How would you compare your products and services to those of the competitors? What are the wholesale and retail costs and profits for each service or product? Who are your current clients and customers?

2) What future products and services do you intend to develop? In what time frames will they be developed? What will be the proposed costs and profits of these new services and products? In the light of these new products, will your company change its focus?

C. **Competitive Analysis:** In this section, you must convince the reader that your company will have some appealing and compelling advantage to prevail over the competition. For example, why do you as an image consultant offer more than an over-the-counter makeup person, store associate, or boutique owner?

D. **Marketing Analysis:** This section lets potential investors know that you have done your research about the people and companies to whom you will be marketing your products and services.

1) What or who are your target markets? How can your markets be divided? By age, income, professional focus? What are the trends and fashions in your markets?

Where is the market going? What other markets do you see your company expanding into?

2) In the marketing analysis, make a list of all the competitive industries and image companies in your area. What is their reputation? What are their products and services? What are their strengths and weaknesses?

3) Who are your customers and clients? Why are they buying image services? What do they need? What are the factors that influence their buying decisions? Which are your biggest markets?

4) Have your surveyed your clients? What feedback have your current clients given you? Have you surveyed clients in your future markets? What do they want and need?

E. **Marketing Plan:** This section is a detailed description of the methods you will use to get your products and services to your clients. Take each target market in turn and outline the marketing strategies for each.

1) What is your pricing strategy? How will you establish a reputation? What will you be known for? What is your image to the public?

2) How will you divide up your marketing budget? What advertising will you do, if any? What networking clubs, associations, and Chambers of Commerce will you join? Image consulting is a relationship business. How will you become known in your community or region? What are the channels you will use to promote your product? (Direct mail, personal contacts, trade associations, newspaper, TV, radio, magazine articles, PR events, Yellow Pages, Web site advertising, newsletter, exhibitor booths, free demonstrations and seminars, telemarketing?)

3) If you use other employees to sell or market your services and products, how will you utilize their services? How will you compensate them?

F. Principals: Anyone who is thinking of investing in your company wants to know who they are dealing with. As the principal, CEO, and sometimes sole proprietor (and sole employee) of your business, YOU become the business. Its success relies on you. It is therefore extremely important that you know your strengths and weaknesses. Do you know what you should be doing personally to grow the business? Where do you need to delegate responsibilities to others?

The strength of the principals and the management team is the key to the success of the company. Become quite at home in selling yourself and promoting your skills and experience. The business plan is not the place to be modest. You will gain self-confidence by going through the process outlined in this section.

1) Summarize your strengths, experience, education, and accomplishments. Do you have an advisory board; if so, who are they and what is their experience? What important contacts do you or they have? Why are you qualified to be the head of an image consulting business?

2) Who will you employ to take on the parts of the business you do not intend to perform?

G. **Financial Information:** Potential investors will be very curious about the current financial status of your business. Make sure that your business plan offers the following information or answers to the following questions:

- What is your current balance sheet?
- What is the point in your business where you break even?
- Show your pro-forma (profit and loss statements) for the next three years:
    — monthly details for the first year
    — quarterly details for the second and third years
- Outline the cash flow projections for the next three years. How did you arrive at those figures?

CHAPTER TWELVE

Balancing Career, Personal Life, and Family

If there were only one way to achieve balance in one's life, we would not need this chapter. Anyone who truly knows how to do this *and* can impart this wisdom to others should be named a saint, for they have discovered both the meaning of life and the ability to bottle it. Each of us leads a multifaceted life, with demands from multiple dimensions. We are constantly experiencing push and pull from all sides. In the business environment, the pace of life is accelerating, and for some it is out of control. Information travels at the speed of a click, opportunities bombard us by the minute, and we have to make choices at a rate never before experienced in history.

Being entrepreneurial image consultants requires that we learn to wear many hats—that of manager, marketer, image consultant, writer, bookkeeper, shopper of clothes (and mundane supplies), administrator, good listener, and counselor to our clients. The life of an image consultant attracts people who are stimulated by change, who are creative, and who have a passion for their work. Although the range and type of services we offer may be similar in most businesses, how we choose to manage and maintain our lives is a completely personal choice.

We are teachers, artisans, business people, and coaches. In order to do what we do well, we must be able to manage change, be comfortable with it, and learn to pilot the ship when the winds shift directions and speed.

The operative verb here is *manage*. Most of the seasoned and successful consultants we interviewed agree that sometimes life just spins out of control. If you are a single parent juggling running a business, raising kids, and budgeting alimony payments and a mortgage, then the last thing you want is to have a client pull out of a contract or your assistant call in sick when you have to attend a school play.

151

If you are married and your husband has to travel for his business to an exotic place and invites you to accompany him, how do you keep your own business going while you are away for the three-week adventure? If you are a new consultant growing your image business while maintaining the day job that financially fuels your new career and also taking classes at night, when do you sleep? If your business is growing too fast and you cannot keep up with the demand, do you work seven days a week and burn the midnight oil? The answers lie in *planning* and *prioritizing*.

We have placed a great deal of emphasis on values, goals, and vision. What is important to you? What do you want to accomplish? What does your ideal business look like? Where are you headed? You will soon realize that all of your decisions are based upon these factors. These questions become your guiding beacons. you're the wisest strategy is to also use them as your anchors. They will help you choose your course of action at any given moment. Your values are likely to shift the least. Your goals and vision will continue to evolve, but your values are intrinsic to your being. When an opportunity knocks on your door, a crisis thwarts your process, and your husband has made plans for dinner, you should choose your actions based upon the options and your values, goals, and vision. *Making it all work for everyone* might be a maxim you could live by.

For example, Karen Brunger, AICI, is a successful image consultant in Toronto, Ontario, Canada. She has a training school, runs a private consulting practice, writes training manuals, teaches at George Brown College, raises a family of three children with her husband, and is a certified practitioner of Holographic Repatterning to individual and corporate clients. In addition, Karen finds time for volunteer participation in professional association work and community projects. When asked how she creates balance, her answer is:

There is no balance. It's impossible!

On a more helpful note, this is how I do it. I create my own expectations and priorities, rather than following the "norm." My three children are independent and can be responsible for their own meals. I have a cleaning crew for the housework, but between times if the children want to make extra money they can do chores. I am now organizing for a chef to provide us with vegetarian meals on a weekly basis. Saturday is "date night" with my husband, and Sunday is "family day." I have people helping me in my business, and this makes a HUGE difference. Anything I don't need to do personally, I delegate. That has been the key to having it all work.

These are the choices that Karen has made for herself, because she and her family are clear about their values and priorities. By giving all the parts of her life their own place and time, the components can coexist and everyone is adequately served.

Many consultants recommend that you begin each day by doing something for yourself, even if it means getting up 30 to 60 minutes earlier. This way, you begin the day having fed your soul some of the food it needs in addition to that bagel and cream cheese for your body. Penny Pilafas, AICI, a corporate image consultant from Pittsburgh, suggests particularly for anyone juggling single parenthood and starting a career:

Always remember to take time for yourself every day. Exercise is important, even if it is just a 20-minute walk, as it refreshes your mind and body, and it clears your head to allow creativity to flow.

By starting your day with you, you have more of yourself to give to your clients and work in the hours to follow. This also reduces any resentment you may develop as a result of devoting endless hours to your business. Before, when you worked for someone else, you could direct this resentment at your job or your boss. Guess who the target is now? Don't turn frustrations in on yourself.

Your work is now a labor of love. It is truly a privilege and an honor to work for yourself and be passionate about your work. You are in the minority. Most people just have a job. As an entrepreneur, your business can become your identity. And especially as image consultants, our work is about expressing our identity. But don't lose your identity to your business.

Evana Maggiore, AICI, a fashion/Feng Shui practitioner in Boston, is always focused on creating harmony and balance as part of both her work and personal life.

> *One way I do this is use my "ME FIRST" method, which I also teach to my clients. I have found that "extreme self-care" (a term borrowed from lifestyle coach Cheryl Richardson) is essential to this approach. By taking the time to focus on MY needs (regular massages, Yoga classes, an occasional day-of-beauty, and at least one day a week reserved for my personal pleasures [shopping, or lunch with friends]), I naturally create more quality time for the rest of my interests and responsibilities. I practice "time abundance" in order to create it. I also made a pact with the universe to live in the NOW, not worrying about what was or will be.*

The pattern that is unfolding is also discipline. To practice what you preach, you must apply your principles to your everyday lifestyle. Setting boundaries for yourself and communicating them to others will actually include others instead of excluding them. Organize a workspace that the children know is not their play space. Allow the voice mail to answer your calls when you are having dinner with your family. These boundaries affect the quality of your life. If you clearly and respectfully state your boundaries, others will respect them, too. If your life is chaotic and you can never seem to meet a deadline, think about this: have you said "no" to anyone this week? Too often we are inclined to say "yes," hoping to please everyone, and we end up pleasing no one.

With the growth of professional coaching, you, too, may be coaching your clients. Learn to be your own coach. Adopt a routine much like that of an athlete training for a competition. It may feel odd at first to put attention on yourself instead of on all the other people to whom you have devoted your time and energy. Once you take on a disciplined routine, it will become part of your lifestyle. It will be as natural as brushing your teeth in the morning. The *"me first"* concept should not be considered selfish. When you travel by airplane, in an emergency you would put the oxygen mask on yourself first, before the children.

This is so you, as the adult, can be fit to take care of the children. We need to stay fit and take care of ourselves in order for us to provide guidance and services to our clients.

Another common challenge that robs us of balance is a failure to separate, physically and mentally, from our work. This is especially true for those of us who work from home. As the business is coming in, we see the results of our labors. We can easily become addicted to doing *more* until we forget that there is another world beyond our wonderful image business. When you are asked by a friend or relative to go out to dinner, do you find yourself answering: *"Later, I have to finish sending out these packages." "I can't stop; I have to call back that client who can't talk freely at his office."* Regretfully, *later* never seems to come. We become caught up in being the only one to bring in the bacon. Yet we love the gratification, the taste of success, and the feeling of the personal reward it brings. We love happy clients. Like any addict, we want more and more until sometimes we lose sight of our life's purpose, or even that we have family and friends. This addictive state is another black hole. The difference with this hole is that you think you have to be in it in order to hold on to your success, but that's not the case. Nor will you realize balance and joy in your life if you stay in that hole.

When your business turns an exciting corner, it's a good idea to revisit your values, goals, and vision. Ask yourself if this is the way you envisioned your success. You may have created the tangible parts, objects, and symbols. But have you created the quality of life you envisioned? If you have not included that in your written declaration of your vision, go back and do it now. After all, you have chosen to pilot your own ship, to take your own path. Have you created a monster? Has this boss become more of a slave driver than the one you left behind?

Catherine Bell, AICI, from Kingston, Ontario, Canada shares her solution to the dilemma:

> *In my multifaceted image consulting business, which continues to grow and demand more hours each year, it is important for me to evaluate where I should be spending my time when at work. It is*

"Make sure that you have vacations, constantly! Everybody needs time to re charge the batteries for the next long drive."
—Jon Michail, AICI

155

obvious that the areas that bring in the most income should be given priority, but when the telephone begins to ring and the e-mails mount up, it is easy to get carried away with low-priority matters that steal valuable time. I have begun to set aside time at the beginning of each week to make a list of income-generating activities and devote quality time to pursuing these each morning when I am most productive. Instead of allowing my business to handle me, I am now handling my business.

Last year, I moved Prime Impressions out of my home into a shared office space with two meeting rooms and a boardroom. Not only did this force me to separate my private time from my business, which is crucial to one's well-being, but it allowed me to expand and simplify my services. In the past, I had to rent space for teaching courses; now I have a boardroom in-house. No matter how businesslike my home office was, the elegantly decorated meeting rooms to which I now have access create a more professional business image in the eyes of my corporate clients. This instills greater confidence in my services and is moving my business forward.

When we are in a state of reaction, we are no longer managing our time creatively. You might spin yourself into reaction when a few normal things happen in an abnormal time frame. For example, a new prospect asks that you send him an information packet by Fed Ex. A moment later a corporate client changes the dates of your program and you have already printed the workbooks with the original date on them. And in the next 15 minutes, another prospect calls asking if you offer a service that is new to you. (Actually you have been thinking of learning it but have never done it.) Now, do you say yes and learn it fast, or lose the opportunity? With this state of affairs, how on Earth can you think clearly enough to make choices? Perhaps your marketing campaign has whirled into motion. Life has a funny way of coming at you at point-blank range. In many instances, we are reacting to the bombardment of life. We will always feel breathless, as if we were in a perpetual state of catching up.

Stephen R. Covey has a chapter in his book *First Things First* that is entitled "Learning from Living." In it he presents a cycle of learning and growth. *As we organize, act, evaluate . . .organize, act, evaluate . . . organize, act and evaluate again, our weeks become repeating cycles of learning and growth.* We create a condition of perpetual motion. We are able to manage this motion more effectively when we evaluate as we go along. It is important to create pauses in the day, week, and month to evaluate our actions and mistakes and learn from them, not be destined to repeat them.

The opposite side of the coin is when you are in a state of doubt and indecision and you fall into *action, paralysis, reaction.* Here you are, at the crossroads without a clue or an ounce of confidence, and you cannot seem to move forward. Recognize this as a red flag and find a coach or a friend to help you back into action. The best way to emerge from writer's block is to keep writing. Choose an action or project that is mundane and will not harm your business if it falls short of expectations, but *just do it.*

You need to prepare for these very common occurrences. There is a form of conscious surrender that you can experience in order to reclaim your steering wheel. Allow yourself to feel thwarted and discouraged from time to time when the results may not reflect your vision. It will not all go perfectly smoothly! Just keep going. If you have ever had the experience of being in a drowning whirlpool, you know that the force of the spiraling water pulls you down. The more you fight it, the more it pulls you down. If you surrender to the natural force of the current, you will naturally and more quickly hit bottom and be able to push yourself up with your own force. Some things just need to go through their intended process. Surrender to the current and you will learn the lesson that awaits you in the next challenge.

Peter Senge in *The Fifth Discipline* writes:

> *Real learning gets to the heart of what it means to be human. Through learning we re-create ourselves. Through learning we become able to do something we never were able to do. Through learning we*

CHAPTER THIRTEEN

Planning for the Future

To know where you are going, start by looking behind you.

The image industry first started in the late 1970s and early 1980s. Before that, "image" for the general public was not a familiar concept, and dress and appearance were akin to fashion, fluctuating with the seasons. Basic principles in dress sense were not widely taught, except at finishing and modeling schools. Color was at the whim of the fashion forecasters, and people either wore basic colors or the colors that were in vogue for the season. When color theories were created and introduced, it became a completely novel experience to learn that your own coloring was best suited to certain colors, and that certain other colors did not suit you at all. Gradually, the theory became accepted as an established image principle, and the whole notion of personal image was born.

For the most part, people did not think in terms of having an "image," or that their appearance influenced perception to any important degree. It was only vaguely appreciated that what you wore mattered to your career. IBM was the only bastion of corporate dress, allowing sales associates to wear blue and white shirts only. Even as late as 1970, hats had to be worn as part of the corporate dress code. Politicians, models, TV personalities, and celebrities were the only likely candidates for an image makeover. The rest of us just wore clothes and hoped that we did not look too terrible!

Then in the 1980s, several forces combined to pave the way for the image industry to emerge. The seasonal color theories made it to the mainstream and swept through the country like a revolution. Everyone had to have their colors done. At the same time, women were entering the workforce in increasing numbers and competing in a man's world. They were on men's turf; they needed to look the part. The suit industry was in its prime, and the dress-for-success look was at a premium.

For the first time women held significant positions in the workforce and had discretionary income to spend. They saw that image mattered to their upward mobility and spent money on their appearance.

The Current Climate

"Behold the turtle. He makes progress only when he sticks his neck out."
—James B. Conant

Today, life in the business world has accelerated with unprecedented velocity. Conventional attitudes and values have changed, and the competition is stiffer than ever. The affluent high-tech companies influenced an anti-suit-and-tie campaign, and a good image seemed to be a less important factor than the next hot idea in building a stellar career. Is image less important than it used to be a decade ago? Hardly. More than ever, people want to be in control of their careers and their lives and are willing to better themselves to arrive there. One of the most effective ways to demonstrate that you own your career or that you are in control of your career path is in your most visible display: your image.

The introduction of business-casual dress in the workplace is almost an oxymoron, two words that ten years ago did not appear in the same sentence, let alone in the same office. As much as it appears to be a benefit to the employees, it has actually brought up some confusion. The employees ask *how do we do it?* And the corporations ask *how do we maintain control of professionalism without losing staff?* The benefit to us is that this widespread confusion presents us with opportunities to go into the workplace and help corporate America get dressed again. We can help redefine the image standards through programs and coaching. The business-casual dress conundrum has also become a marketing vehicle, enabling us to reinvent standards of professionalism, etiquette, business protocol, and the human aspect of corporate identity. We can coach employees on how to dress appropriately so that they do not abuse and lose the benefit. The opportunities are limitless.

Appearance, adornment, and image have always been status symbols—communicating messages and signifying wealth, prestige, and power. Whatever happens in dress-casual, business suits, body piercing, or silver domes, appearance and image will always produce its status symbols. People who wear or own these symbols will be demonstrating their rank at the top of their community. This is unlikely to change, even if the status symbol of the moment of a particular community is grunge, punk, tattoos, kilts, or period costume.

What Are Some of the Emerging Markets?

As image consultants, we can look to see where the next emerging markets will be. The answer is: wherever people have an opportunity to raise their standards and take control of their circumstances.

Women in Business

In business in the U.S.A., Canada, Japan, and Europe, the female market is full of promise for image consultants. Women are taking on positions of power and prestige. Instead of competing with men, they will soon be competing with other women for the top jobs. That situation will mean looking the best and honing skills that are valued by women: appearance, connectivity, collaboration, and communication. Our services should reflect this increasingly pressing future need. Again, if women are heading up corporations, image consultants will be in demand to enhance external and internal image, improve the look of uniforms, encourage higher standards of dress and appearance, and use communication and image training as a way to increase self-confidence and personal effectiveness.

Latin American countries face the same evolution where women, once considered less-than-competent business people, are holding their own in increasing numbers and becoming a force in the business world. There, they are interested in women looking fashionable and feminine, so clothes, makeup, and hair styling will always be of great importance.

The Political Scene

For years, American business and political machines have used consultants to mold the image of political candidates. In Latin American, Asian, and third-world countries, there is a growing trend to change the face and shape of politics as democratic systems become stronger. Image consultants are being hired to prepare candidates for presentation to the voting constituents. Political hopefuls are taught principles of strategic dressing— the appropriate colors, fabrics, and patterns to wear onstage or on-camera—body language, and acting techniques. Speaking and media training skills are also part of the candidate's essential survival kit. People need to identify with the candidate, yet they only have sound bites on television from which to form an opinion. Taken from this standpoint, the visual, verbal, and nonverbal communication "packaging" of a candidate has become vitally important to success.

National Manners and International Etiquette

As the world seems to shrink, we travel to far-flung reaches of the planet and need to know the mores and customs of the countries we visit, whether for business or pleasure. Business and social etiquette will become increasingly important as organizations spin their international webs. In the United States, we will be placing a greater importance on manners, social interaction, and civility. Given enough time, there will be a swing away from casual manners, loutish behavior, and lack of discipline. Parents raised in the sixties are already seeing the fruits of their permissive generation—children are leaving school unable to read or write; rage and abuse are left unpunished; and anarchy reigns in classrooms, as evident in tragic shootings. We as etiquette consultants are already in demand to teach children manners and correct behavior. What was once the job of the parent and the school has become a social responsibility that requires new skills from outside the existing systems. We have the opportunity to contribute to society by teaching values, social skills, and communication skills to help build self-esteem and pride. We can also develop programs to support educators trying to manage conflict resolution in the classroom. Grooming today's youth prepares them to become our future leaders.

The Corporate Market

If we intend to help corporations, we need to get a grasp on the future trends and needs of the corporate world. We must fit our message into the big picture and the bottom line. We have to demonstrate how visual, verbal, and nonverbal communication become components of the identity and culture of an organization. They help build its competitive edge. Competition for and retention of talent will be one of the major challenges facing the corporate world in this decade. To retain the best and brightest, an organization has to woo employees with useful benefits. Employees will also stay with an organization if they are trained and developed at every stage, and are aware of the contribution they are making. A company with high visibility and a powerful corporate identity will be more successful in attracting top-notch personnel. Our work helps build the corporate identity. If we teach etiquette, business practices, and verbal and nonverbal communication, we are also contributing to the climate of the corporate culture.

The Special-Size Market

This market is growing rapidly. Fashion has neglected this market for many years, imposing unrealistic body image standards suggested by the fashion magazines, the media, and clothing in the stores. Clients with special-size needs—such as plus size and petites—are incredibly loyal and in need of our services and products. The introduction of magazines and clothing catalogues indicate manufacturers are finally waking up to this opportunity.

The African-American, Hispanic, and Asian Markets

These markets have also been sorely neglected over the years. In terms of products, these markets are very interested in image, cosmetics, skin care, and hair care products. Color analysis is also of interest, and more specialized due to the complexity of skin tones. These groups are now competing for the same jobs and professional positions as Caucasians, and are just as willing to invest in their appearance and personal development. Evidence of the potential success of this market is apparent in the number of fashion, lifestyle, and business magazines and special cosmetics lines that have emerged in the last few years.

The Senior Market

This is another excellent market to approach. Seniors today are retiring at a younger age, and with more discretionary income than in previous decades. Many travel extensively, are starting second careers and second relationships, are eager to express themselves

"If you don't like something, change it; if you can't change it, change the way you think about it."
— Mary Engelbreit

163

through their image, and are willing to pay for services. They will be interested in clothing, image services, skin care and cosmetics, and travel wardrobes.

Sports Personalities

Sportspersons can receive an enormous amount of media visibility. In addition to their athletic success, many seek to be selected for endorsements. This involves positioning as a successful athlete and team player, role model, and spokesperson. They need to be able to speak in public, uphold an image, and represent properly the product or company employing them. Many do not have prior exposure to speaking skills, etiquette, and image. They need to be coached in these skills, and in how to field the media in interviews. In addition, they need clothing to make themselves presentable and position themselves for endorsement.

Organizational Branding

Organizations have found that adopting a brand and identifying their "brand promise" is a useful marketing tool to engage and inspire the public to buy their product—not only from the head, but also from the heart. We as image consultants can play an important part in creating and developing an organization's brand.

Branding is beyond identity; it has little to do with the actual product, the price, or the market share. It has everything to do with the perceived value, the perceived quality, and the feeling one has about the product or company. Brands are not generic, nor are they a commodity. Brands feel familiar, well known, and comfortable. They appeal to your mind and, most importantly, your heart and emotions. Brands are known for something other than their names. They are often known by a slogan ("When you care enough to send the very best", Hallmark), a symbol (Apple), or logo (Lacoste Alligator), packaging (Tiffany), their geography (Channel), or a representation (Volvo for safety, Coca-Cola for energy, smiles and happiness). The things surrounding the product, such as value, performance, excellence, quality, comfort and ease provide the brand, not the thing itself (Lexus). It is the singular distinction and the halo effect or aura surrounding the product that establishes the brand. As Tom Peters says, "Sell the Sizzle, not the Steak."

The work of consultants who design and implement an organization's brand may include:

- Assessments of the current state of the organization and the intended goal
- Analysis of the image expectation of the organization by its public
- Analysis of attitudes and human climate that may pose challenges or be a support, including internal organizational politics
- Understanding of communication channels and the hierarchical framework already in place
- Identification and allocation of resources needed to implement the goal (funds, labor, skills, timing)
- Team building, team management experience and organizational development skills
- Project management skills including time management

Personal Branding

If the branding concept can work for an organization, it can also work for an individual. People are realizing the value of branding themselves to achieve a certain aura or charisma and are engaging the services of an image consultant to help. Charismatic people are those who influence and attract others, gain promotions, and seem to lead charmed lives. Not to be confused with "con men", manipulators or social climbers, people with strong personal brands have worked hard to perfect an image that represents who they are in the world. Their visual identity, verbal and nonverbal communication skills are all impeccable representations of their vision and values in life. They walk the talk and they know what that talk is.

Successful image consultants know only too well that clothes and body language express clear messages. We can help people understand and achieve a personal brand by improving and enhancing their natural talents, and linking their external appearance to their internal persona. They can then align their outer, visual message with their inner qualities and goals.

A personal brand ensures that an individual stands out above the pack. This becomes a priceless tool, especially when the competition is fierce. A quality wardrobe and style, excellent comportment, posture and demeanor help project a person's capabilities and personal qualities. A clearly defined and appropriately expressed personal identity can serve to market an individual as the obvious choice for promotion and career advancement. Etiquette, communication and protocol skills undoubtedly also help individuals handle challenges in their personal and professional lives.

As image consultants, we have the ability to equip our clients with the right tools. To be effective we must also coach our clients to be authentic and at the same time understand the constantly changing rules of the business game. In the future, this concept will become increasingly important and we must be ready to fill the need.

Branding Yourself as an Image Consultant

The actual services we offer now and in the future may not differ greatly from those offered over the past decade. How we package, position and promote our services is critical. We must answer for ourselves, *"What is the image of the image consulting profession?"* The perceptions that clients have of us today as professionals are very different from twenty years ago. In response, many image consultants have shifted their own perception, and may have adopted any of the following titles: image coach or consultant, visual communications manager, perception manager, personal communications trainer or image strategist.

To present yourself as an image consultant, coach or trainer, you must go through the same assessment process that a large company experiences when branding a product. This means answering similar questions about your product or service, your customer and his expectations. You are your product and your best sales tool; in essence a very demonstration of the results and benefits of your work. From business cards, electronic communications and press kits down to your wardrobe and appearance, everything must be congruent to ensure that everything you do, say and present to your public represents your personal brand.

Epilogue: Where Do We Go from Here?

Educating ourselves is vitally important. As image consultants to the general public, we will need to keep up with the current fashions in dress and appearance. We will also need to master human skills. If we want to increase our value to corporations, our worth depends on the extent to which we can first, set trends and standards, and second, empower people to take responsibility for and transform their own image. This change can stem from the use of transformational methodologies: research-based coaching and assessment tools that enable a consultant to empower individuals and groups. Some of the issues these tools are designed to address are listening and speaking skills, customer service, team building, and managing change.

As an industry, we must keep raising our own standards. Our top credentials and our bottom credentials must be higher. We must continue to do research and develop an even greater arsenal of proof that image matters, not merely on a superficial level. We must be able to demonstrate that image represents quality and high standards through and through. If we document the results of our work, we can raise public awareness of the impact of image in personal and professional relationships. If we measure an increase in the bottom line as a result of improved customer service, and if we show a decrease in employee attrition due to the enhancement of employee services, we can then demonstrate our value to our clients. And if we help our individual clients strengthen their self-esteem, save time and money through our services, and prepare them to deal effectively with the ups and downs of life, we are also contributing to society.

We encourage you to use your experience, educate yourself, and take on image consulting as a career. Deal with perpetual roadblocks, overcome diversity, and keep going. From a personal standpoint, you will be working in the extremely rewarding fields of creativity, beauty, and aesthetics. In no other profession will you be able to see so clearly the difference you are making: you'll be helping people with their self-confidence and being part of a force that shapes their future.

SECTION 3
Where Do You Go for Help?

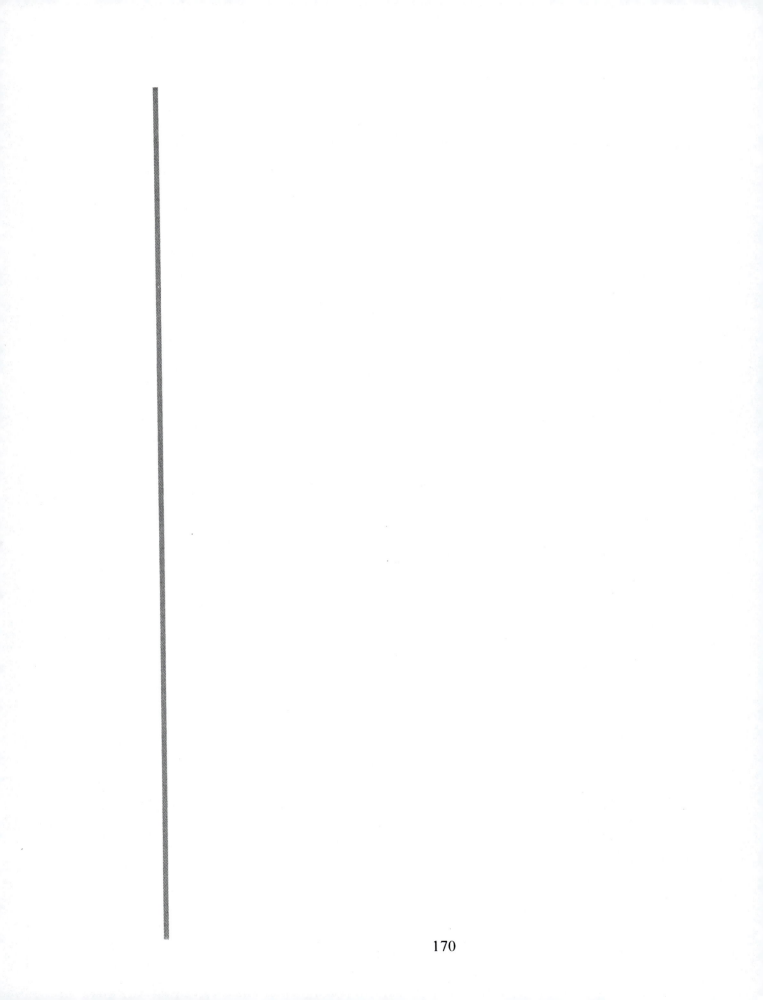

Professional Associations and Business Development Resources

American Association of Home Based Businesses (AAHBB) P.O. Box 10023 Rockville, MD 20849	T 800.447.9710 www.aahbb.org
The Association for Women in Communications 1244 Ritchie Highway, Suite 6 Arnold, MD 21012-1877	T 410.544.7442 F 410.544.4640 EM nancy@womcom.org www.womcom.org
American Home Business Association 4505 S. Wasatch Blvd., Suite 140 Salt Lake City, UT 84124	www.homebusiness.com T 800 664.2422 F 800 273.2399
American Management Association 1601 Broadway New York, NY 10019	T 212.586.8100/ 800 262.9699 F 212 903.8168 www.amanet.org
American Marketing Association 311 S. Wacker Drive, Suite 5800 Chicago, IL 60606	T 312.542.9000 800 262.1150 www.marketingpower.com
American Society of Training and Development 1640 King Street, Box 1443 Alexandria, VA 22313	T 703.683.8100 F 703 683.1523 www.astd.org
American Woman's Economic Development Corporation (AWED) 216 East 45 Street, 10th floor New York, NY 10017	T 917 368.6100 www.awed.org
Association of Business Support Services, Inc. 5852 Oak Meadow Drive Yorba Linda, CA 92886	T 800.237.1462 / 714 695.9398 F 714 779.8106 www.abssi.org

Association of Image Consultants International - **AICI**
12300 Ford Road, Suite 1345
Dallas, TX 75234
	T 877.247.3319
	   972.755.1503
	F 972.755.2561
	   www.aici.org

Center for Entrepreneurial Management, Inc. 457 Washington Street New York, NY 10013	T 212.633.0060 F 212.633.0063 www.ceoclubs.org
Home Business Institute, Inc. PO Box 480215 Delray Beach, FL 33448	T 561.865.0865 / 888 DIALHBI
Idea Café (Information and resources for small-business professionals, especially those just starting out)	www.ideacafe.com
Khera Communications, Inc. Sample agreements, advice 9700 Great Seneca Highway Rockville, MD 20850	www.morebusiness.com T 240 453.8499 F 240 453.6208

Landmark Education 353 Sacramento Street, suite 200 San Francisco, CA 94111	T 415 981.8850 F 415 616.2411 www.landmarkeducation.com
Marketing Research Association 1344 Silas Deane Highway, Suite 306 (PO Box 230) Rocky Hill, CT 06067	T 860.257.4008 F 860.257.3990 www.mra-net.org
National Association of Female Executives (NAFE) 30 Irving Place New York, NY 10003	T 800.636.6233 T 800 634.NAFE www.nafe.com
National Association of Professional Organizers (NAPO) P.O. Box 140 Austin, TX 78714	T 512.206.0151 (nat'l office) F 512 454.3036 www.napo.net
National Association of Women Business Owners 1595 Spring Hill Road, suite 330 Vienna, VA 22182	T 800 55 NAWBO 703 506 3268 www.nawbo.org
National Minority Business Council, Inc. 25 West 45 Street, suite 301 New York, NY 10036	T 212.997.4753 F 212 997.5102 www.nmbc.org
National Speakers Association (NSA) 1500 South Priest Drive Tempe, AZ 85281	T 480.968.2552 F 480.968.0911 www.nsaspeaker.org
Small Business Administration–SBA Online 409 Third Street, SW Washington, DC 20416	T 800.827.5722 www.sba.gov
Small Business Network 10451 Mill Run Circle, Suite 400 Owings Mills, MD 21117	T 410.581.1373
Small Business Service Bureau 554 Main Street P.O. Box 15014 Worcester, MA 01615-0014	T 508.756.3513 F 508.791.4709 www.sbsb.com
SOHO America (small office home office) P.O. Box 941 Hurst, TX 76053-0941	www.soho.org
Toastmasters International Box 9052 Mission Viejo, CA 92690	T 949.858.8255 F 949.858.1207 www.toastmasters.org

Marketing, Public Relations, and Networking

Networking Organizations

Business Network International 199 South Monte Vista Avenue, Suite 6 San Dimas, CA 91773-3080	T 909.305.1818 /800 825.8280 F 909 305.1811 www.bni.com
Leads Club P.O. Box 279 Carlsbad, CA 92018-0279	T 760.434.3761 800.783.3761 www.leadsclub.com
LeTip, International PO Box 178130 San Diego, CA 92117	T 800.255.3847 F 858.490.2744 www.letip.org

Media, Mailing Lists, and Promotions

Advertising and Public Relations for a Small Business by Diane Bellavance	DBA Books Boston
Advertising and Sales Promotion: Cost Effective Techniques for Your Small Business by William Brannen	Prentice-Hall
American Business Directories 5711 South 86th Circle P.O. Box 273478 Omaha, NE 68127 They publish: • American Consumer Lists • Lists of 9 Million Businesses • Online Information Network • Nationwide Directory of Business	
Bacon's Information Services Bacon's Media Directories 332 South Michigan Avenue, Suite 900 Chicago, IL 01604	T 800.621.0561 312.922.2400 www.baconsinfo.com
Burelle's Information Services 75 East Northfield Road Livingston, NJ 07039	T 800 631.1160 www.burelles.com

Business Wire 1990 S. Bundy Los Angeles, CA 90025 (newswire service)	T 310.820.9473
Corbin Data Management Systems Debbie Corbin 1594 York Avenue, Suite 21 New York, NY 10028 (database design and management)	T 212.988.5612 F 212.988.2079 EM Corbinmanagement@aol.com
Databases (2000)	www.isleuth.com
Directory of Mailing List Companies P.O. Box 635 Nyack, NY 10960	T 914.358.6213
DL Graphics Diane Holleran 8454 Coventry Drive Allison Park, PA 15101-3361 (print, PowerPoint design, books etc.)	T 412.367.3848 F 412.367.1842 EM holleran@usaor.net
Dun's National Business List Dun's Marketing Services 3 Sylvan Way Parsippany, NJ 07054	T 973.605.6000
Essentials of Advertising Strategy by Don Schult	Crain Books
Gale's Directory of Directories Gale Directory of Databases Gale Research 27500 Drake Road Farmington Hills, MI 48331-3535	T 800.8774253 www.gale.com
The Hugo Dunhill Mailing Lists Catalog 30 East 33rd Street, 12th Floor New York, NY 10016	T 800.223.6454 F 212 213.9245 www.hdml.com
Mail Tools Database Companion by MySoftware Company 2197 East Bayshore Road Palo Alto, CA 94803	T 650.473.3600 www.mysoftware.com
My Advanced Mailing-List & Address Book by MySoftware Company 2197 East Bayshore Road Palo Alto, CA 94803	T 650.473.3600 www.mysoftware.com
News USA 198 Van Buren Street, Suite 420 Herndon, VA 20170 (newswire service)	T 800 355.9500 703.834.1818
Oxbridge Communications 150 Fifth Avenue, Suite 302 New York, NY 10011	T 800.955.0231 www.mediafinders.com

PR Newswire 810 7th Avenue, 35th Floor New York, NY 10019	T 800.832.5522 www.prnewswire.com
The Polk Mailing List Catalog R.L. Polk & Co. 26955 Northwestern Highway, Suite 100 Southfield, MI 48034	T 248.728.7000
Research Institute for Small and Emerging Businesses RISEbusiness	T 202.628.8382 www.riseb.org EM rise@bellatlantic.net
SalesLeads USA by American Business Information 5711 South 86th Circle P.O. Box 27347 Omaha, NE 68127	T 402.593.4593 F 402.331.1505 800.555.5335 www.salesleadsusa.com www.listbazaar.com
Standard Rate and Data Service 1700 Higgins Road Des Plains, IL 60018	T 847.256.6067 800.851.7737 www.srds.com available in libraries
Writer's Digest F & W Publications 1507 Dana Avenue Cincinnati, OH 45207	T 513.531.2222 www.FWPublications.com

On Line Yellow Pages

BigBook	www.bigbook.com
Bigfoot	www.bigfoot.com
BigYellow	www.bigyellow.com
Four11	www.four11.com
GTE Super Pages	www.superpages.gte.net
NewYellow	www.newyellow.com
ON'VILLAGE	www.onvillage.com
Who Where?	www.whowhere.com

Recommended Reading

Beauty, Color, Fashion and Image Books

Always in Style by Doris Pooser	Crisp Publications
Best Impressions, How to Gain Professionalism, Promotion and Profit by Dawn E. Waldrop	BookMasters Inc.
Beyond Business Casual by Ann Marie Sabath	Career Press
Beyond the Color Explosion by Renae Knapp	Rainy Day Publishing
Business Casual Made Easy by Ilene Amiel and Angie Michael	Business Casual Publications LC
Casual Power by Sherry Maysonave	Bright Books

The Chic Simple Series
   • *Men's Wardrobe*
   • *Women's Wardrobe*
   • *Workclothes*
by Kim Johnson Gross & Jeff Stone
	www.chicsimple.com

Clothes and the Man by Alan Flusser	Villard Books
Color and Human Response by Faber Birren	Chronical Books
Color Me Beautiful, Looking Your Best by Mary Spillane & Christine Sherlock	Ballantine Books
Color with Style by Donna Fujii	Graphic-sha Publishing Co., Ltd.
The Color Consultants Handbook by Debra Lindquist	EM ahha59a@prodigy.com
Dress Casually for Success for Men by Mark Weber and the Van Heusen Creative Design Organization	McGraw Hill
Dress Code by Toby Fischer-Mirken	Clarkson Potter
Dress for Success by John Malloy	Warner Books
Dressing the Whole Person-9 ways to Create Harmony & Balance in Your Wardrobe by Evana Maggiore	Mansion Publishing Ltd

Essential Self, Essential Style, by Alyce Parsons, Kathy Hurley, Theodore Donson	Wind Walker Press EM- ParsonsUS@aol.com
Everything Need to Know About Color But Were Afraid to Ask by Sharon Chrisman and Debra Lindquist	EM Smchrisman@aol.com
Formulas for Dressing the Whole Person (workbook) by Louise Elerding & Evana Maggiore	EM Lelerding@aol.com
Fashion Secrets Mother Never Told You by Ginger Burr	www.totalimageaconsultants.com
Flatter Your Figure by Jan Larkey	Simon & Schuster
Forty over Forty by Brenda Kinsel	Wildcat Canyon Press
Image Consulting for the 21st Century by Brenda York-McDaniel	Academy of Fashion & Image
Image Matters, First Steps on the Journey to Your Best Self, by Lauren Solomon	www.Lsimage.com
The Indispensable Guide to Classic Men's Clothing by Josh Karlen & Christopher Sulavik	Tatra Press
In the Dressing Room with Brenda By Brenda Kinsel	Wildcat Canyon Press
Learning Curves by Michelle Weston, Michael Sheldon	Crown Publishers
Living In Color by Renae Knapp	Lighthouse Publishing Group
Looking Good by Nancy Nix-Rice	Palmer/Pletch
Managing Your Image Potential by Catherine Bell, AICI	EM image@kos.net www.webwoods.com/prime
Mastering Your Professional Image by Diane Parente and Stephanie Peterson	Image Development and Management Inc.
Maximum Style by Perry Garfinkel, Brian Chichester	Men's Health
Plus Style by Suzan Nanfeldt	Fashion Institute of Technology 212 217.7717
The Power of Color by Dr. Morton Walker	Avery Publishing Group
Five Steps to Professional Presence by Susan Bixler	G.P. Putnam's Sons

My Bride Guide by Judith Ann Graham	Barricade Press www.myweddingmyway.com
The New Professional Image by Susan Bixler	G.P. Putnam's Sons
Projecting a Positive Image by Marilyn Pincus	Barron's
Secrets of a Fashion Therapist by Betty Halbreich & Sally Wadyka	Cliff Street Books
Suit Yourself by Tim Meehan	J.T. Meehan Publishing
Things a Man Should Know About Style by Scott Omeliank & Ted Allen	
Triumph of Individual Style by Carla Mathis and Helen Villa Connor	Fairchild Books
Universal Style for Men by Alyce Parsons and Diane Parente	EM parsonsUS@aol.com
Wardrobe Strategies for Women by Judith Rasband	Delmar Publishers
The Way We Look, Dress and Aesthetics by Marilyn Revell Delong	Fairchild Publications
What's My Style by Alyce Parsons with Allison L. Better	EM parsonsUS@aol.com
Your Image Builds Business Success, By Jon Michail	Image Group International

Business Development and Growth Books

Abundance Marketing, by Jon Michail	Image Group International www.imagegroup.com.au
Best Impressions, How to Gain Professionalism, Promotion & Profit By Dawn E. Waldrop	Best Impressions, Cleveland, Ohio ISBN 0-9655742-3-7
Coaching for Commitment by Dennis C. Kinlaw	Pfeiffer & Company
Encyclopedia of Associations	Gale Research
The Entrepreneur and Small Business Problem Solver: An Encyclopedic Reference and Guide by William Cohen	John Wiley & Sons, Inc

Getting Business to Come to You by Paul and Sarah Edwards & Laura Clampitt Douglass	Tarcher/Putnum Books
How to Gain the Professional Edge by Susan Morem	Better Books
How to Get Your Point Across in 30 Seconds or Less by Milo O. Frank	Pocket Books / Simon Schuster
How to Work a Room by Susan RoAne	Warner
Masters of Networking by Ivan R Misner, Ph.D., & Don Morgan, M.A.	www.mastersofnetworking.com
Maximum Achievement by Brian Tracey	Fireside Books
Maximizing Profits in Small and Medium-Sized Businesses by Jerome Braverman	Van Nostrand Reinhold Co. Inc
Mentoring: A Success Guide for Mentors and Proteges by Floyd Wickman and Terri Sjodin	McGraw Hill
Mentoring: Confidence in Finding a Mentor & Becoming One by Bobb Biehl	Broadman and Holman Publishers
Minding Your Own Small Business by Nancy Holt, Joe Shuchat, and Mary Lewis Regal	CDC Education and Human Development, Inc. Washington, DC
The Organizer-Secrets and Systems from the World's Top Executive Assistants by Anna-Carin Jean	
Personal Coaching for Results: How to Mentor and Inspire Others to Amazing Growth by Luis E. Tice, Joyce Quick & Lou Tice	Thomas Nelson
The Portable Coach by Thomas J. Leonard	Scribner
Projecting a Positive Image, by Marilyn Pincus	Barron's Educational Series, Inc.
The Secrets to Savvy Networking by Susan RoAne	Warner
The 7 Habits of Highly Effective People by Stephen Covey	Simon & Schuster
Small Business Financing	American Bankers Association

Soloing: Realizing Your Life's Ambition by Harriet Rubin	
Starting Your Own Business by Jan Norman	Upstart Publishing
The Streetwise Guide To Starting & Managing a Business **by Bob Adams**	WWW.businesstown.com
Trademark: How to Name Your Business and Product by Kate McGrath and Stephen Elias	Nolo Press
Transitions: Making Sense of Life's Changes, by William Bridges	Perseus Books
Understanding Money Sources SBA	Small Business Administration
Working from Home by Paul and Sarah Edwards	Tarcher/Putnum
The Working Solo Sourcebook by Terri Lonier	WWW.workingsolo.com

Presentations, Speaking and Protocol Books

Business Protocol by Jan Yager	John Wiley & Sons, Inc.
Complete Business Etiquette by Barbara Pachter & Marjorie Brody	Prentice Hall
Do's and Taboos of Public Speaking by Roger E. Axtell	John Wiley & Sons
How to Be a Working Actor by Mari Lyn Henry and Lynn Rogers	Watson-Guptill Publishers
Intercultural Business by Arthur H. Bell, Ph.D., & Gary G. Williams Ph.D.	Barron's
Kiss, Bow or Shake Hands by Terri Morrison	Adams Media Group
Navigating Cross Country Ethics by Eileen Morgan	Butterworth Heinemann
Please Understand Me: Character & Temperament Types by David Keirsey and Marilyn Bates	Prometheus Nemesis Book Company
Powerful Communication Skills by Colleen McKenna	Career Press

Simply Sophisticated by Suzanne Munshower	The Summit Group
Smart Moves by Sam Deep and Lylle Sussman	Addison-Wesley Publishing Company, Inc.
Speak and Grow Rich by Dottie and Lilly Walters	Prentice-Hall
You Look Great, but How Do You Sound? By Dr. June Johnson	Management Strategies Inc.
When the Little Things Count by Barbara Pachter	Marlow & Company
A Woman's Guide to the Language of Success by Phyllis Mindell, Ed.D.	Prentice Hall

Trade Publications

Business@Home magazine	www.gohome.com
Dearborn Publishing Small-business books	www.dearborn.com

The Image Update
Quarterly AICI Magazine
12300 Ford Road, suite 1345
Dallas, TX 75234
	T 877.247.3319
	    972.755.1503
	F 972.755.2561
	    www.aici.org

The Pricing Advisor 3277 Roswell Road, #620 Atlanta, GA 30305	T 404.252.5708
Self Employment Survival Newsletter P.O. Box 2137 Naperville, IL 60567	T 708.717.4188
Woman's Wear Daily	Fairchild Publications

Magazines

Business

Black Enterprise	www.blackenterprise.com
Entrepreneur	www.entrepreneur.com
Fast Company	www.fastcompany.com
Forbes	www.forbes.com
Hispanic	www.hisp.com
Hispanic Business	www.hispanicbusiness.com
House of Business	www.houseofbusinessdirect.com
Inc.	www.inc.com.
Smart Money	www.smartmoney.com
Working Woman	www.workingwoman.com

Fashion

Bazaar	www.bazaar.com
Black Elegance	www.starloggroup.com
Ebony	www.ebony.com
Elle	www.elle.com
Essence	www.essence.com
GQ	www.gq.com
Glamour	www.glamour.com
InStyle	www.instylemag.com
Latina	www.latina.com
Marie Claire	www.heartsmags.com
More	www.moremag.com
Town and Country	www.hearstmags.com
Vogue	www.vogue.com
W	www.fairchild.com

Lifestyle and Special Interest

B. Smith Style	www.bsmithstyle.com
Esquire	www.esquire.com
Feng Shui	www.fengshui-manazine.com
House and Garden	www.condenet.com/mags/hg
Knitters	www.knittinguniverse.com
Martha Stewart Living	www.marthastewart.com
Men's Health	www.menshealth.com
O (by Oprah Winfrey)	www.oprah.com
Real Simple	www.realsimple.com
Tattler	www.tatler.co.uk
Threads	www.threadsmagazine.com
Traveler of Conde Nast	www.condenast.com
Travel & Leisure	www.travelandleisure.com
Vanity Fair	www.vanityfair.com
Wallpaper	www.wallpaper.com

Consulting Products and Tools

At Ease, Inc. 119 East Court Street Cincinnati, OH 45202	T 1 800 873-9909 513 241-5216 www.corporateetiquette.com
Australian Image Company PO. Box 3075, The Pines Doncaster East, Victoria Australia, 3109	T 61-3-9841-7197 F 61-3-9841-7297 EM taic@websurf.net.au www.taic.com.au
Color Me a Season 2901 Camby Road Antioch, CA 94509	T 800.692.6567 / 925 778.2626 F 925 778.0184 www.colormeaseason.com
Color Style & Carla Mathis Designs 1035 Tehama Avenue Menlo Park, CA 94025	T 650 321.5997 F 650 321.1168 www.Carlamathis.com
Conselle Institute of Image Management 7052 University Station Provo, UT 84602-7052	T 801.224.1207 www.conselle.com
Color Profiles LTD -The Total Look 3011 S. Josephine Denver, CO 80210	T 303.759.8471 F 303 758.5186 EM AHHA59A@PRODIGY.COM
Color Quest 1330 Leyden, Suite 135 Denver, CO 80220	T 303.329.0095 F 303 329.0095 colorquest@myexcel.com
DominiQue IsbecQue International 173 West 78 Street Penthouse A New York, NY 10024-6703	T 212.595-0917 F 212 595.0841 EM Qdisbecque@aol.com
Bridal Beauti (cosmetics) Judith Ann Graham 134 East 64 Street- studio 3B New York, NY 10021	T 212 688.3202 866 81BRIDE
The ImageMaker, Inc. 348 Cool Springs Boulevard Franklin, TN 37067	T 615.771.7258 / 888 845.5600 F 615.376.9891 EM optimist44@aol.com www.imagemaker1.com
International Image, Inc. 1233 Dogwood Drive Forth Worth, TX 76126	T 800.704.6243 F 817.249.5407 EM intimage@flash.net
International Image Institute 1644 Bayview Road, Suite 1318 Toronto, Ontario M4G 3C2 Canada	T 416.809.4321 F 905.738.8564 EM kbrunger@idirect.com http://webhome.idirect.com/~kbrunger/
London Image Institute 4279 Roswell Road, Suite-102, PMB-318 Atlanta, GA 30342	T 404.255.0009 F 404.303.8818 EM Lynnemarks@aol.com www.londonimageinstitute.com

Sandy Moore- Image Matters Consulting 3724 NE 134 Avenue Portland, Oregon 97230	T 503 256.1496 sandy@yourimagematters.biz
Self Incorporated 5307 Beechwood Pt. Court Midlothian, VA 23112	T 804.739.1714 EM strong@erols.com www.selfinc-presentations.com www.mindspring.com/~lei/self
Your New Image 1961 Oakmont Terrance Coral Springs, FL 33071	T 954.755.7933 F 954.755.1452

Consulting Services/Training

Appearance Designers 18951 Ansley Place Saratoga, CA 95070-3572	T/F 408.253.0272 EM colorbycoralyn@yahoo.com
Color Design Systems 1310 Garden Lane Menlo Park, CA 94025-5569	T 650.328.4494 F 650.325.5237 EM Smchrisman@aol.com
Color Education Resources P.O. Box 7704 New York, NY 10116	T 212.564.3082 F 212 564.3082
Conselle Institute of Image Management P.O. Box 7052 University Station Provo, UT 84602-7052	T 801.224.1207 F 801.226.6122 EM Judith@conselle.com www.conselle.com
DominiQue IsbecQue International 173 West 78th Street, PH-A New York, NY 10024-6703	T 212.595.0917 F 212.595.0841 EM Qdisbecque@aol.com
Donna Fuji Institute 2474 Washington Street, Suite 102 San Francisco, CA 94115	T 415.922.9000 F 415.474.4999 EM donna@donnafuji.com www.donnafuji.com
Fashion Institute of Technology (F.I.T.) Seventh Avenue at 27th Street New York, NY 10001-5992	T 212.217.7715 F 212.217.7176 EM seminars@sfitva.cc.fitsuny.edu
George Brown College 200 King Street East Toronto, Ontario, Canada	T 416.415.2000 www.gbrownc.on.ca
Carolyn Gustafson, Inc. Image Strategy for Men & Women 135 East 54th Street New York, NY 10022	T 212.755.4456 F 212.421.0733 EM CG4Image@aol.com www.ImageStrategy.com

Image Group International 47 Darling Street South Yarra, VIC 3141 Australia	T 61 3 9820 4449 www.imagegroup.com.au
Image On The Go 620 Park Road Lansdale, PA 19446	T 215.699.6308 800.822.5106 EM IOTGCindy@aol.com
Image Resource Group 7804 Wincanton Court Falls Church, VA 22043	T 703.560.3950 F 703.573.8904 EM rginc@earthlink.net home.earthlink.net/~irginc
Institute for Image Management Suite 13, 209 Toorak Road South Yarra Vic 3141 Australia	T 613.9824.0420 F 613.9827.3119 EM info@imagegroup.com.au www.imagegroup.com.au
International Image Institute 1644 Bayview Road, Suite 1318 Toronto, Ontario M4G 3C2 Canada	T 416.809.4321 F 905.738.8564 EM kbrunger@idirect.com www.imageinstitute.com
London Image Institute 4279 Roswell Road, Suite-102, PMB-318 Atlanta, GA 30342	T 404.255.0009 F 404.303.8818 EM Lynnemarks@aol.com www.londonimageinstitute.com
Image Group International 47 Darling Street South Yarra, VIC 3141 Australia	T +61 3 9820.4449 F +61 3 9820.4441 EM info@imagegroup.com.au
The ImageMaker, Inc. 348 Cool Springs Blvd. Franklin, TN 37067	T 615.771.7258 F 615.376.9891 EM optimist44@aol.com
Renae Knapp Color Institute 3857 Birch Street #247 Newport Beach, CA 92660	T 949.551.9500 F 949.251.1424 EM rkci@earthlink.net
Style and Color Education Resources The Australian Image Company P.O. Box 3075, The Pines Doncaster East, Victoria Australia 3109	T 61.3.984.7197 F 61.3.9841.7297 EM taic.websurf.net.au www.taic.com.au
Universal Style & Associates 15450 Banyon Lane Monte Sereno, CA 95030	T 408.395.0799 F 408.395.8499 EM ParsonsUS@aol.com

Direct Selling Resources

Amway	www.amway.com
BeautiControl Carrolton, Texas	www.beauticontrol.com
Beauty for all Seasons	www.beautyforallseasons.com
Carlisle Collection 16 East 52 Street New York, NY 10022	212.246.4275 www.carlislecollection.com
Color Me Beautiful 14000Thunderbolt Place, suite E Chantilly, VA 20151	1.800.COLORME F 888.867.8415 www.colormebeautiful.com
Color Me A Season 2401 Camby Road Antioch, CA 94509	1.800.692.6567 F 925.778. 184 www.colormeaseason.com
Direct Selling Association	www.dsa.org
Doncaster Rutherfordton, NC	1.800.669.3662 www.doncsaster.com
French Rags 11500 Tennessee Avenue Los Angeles. CA 90064	800.347.52.70 www.frenchrags.com
Juliana Collezione 1431 Broadway, 10th floor New York, NY 10018	212.575.8800 www.julianaonline.com
Nuskin	www.nuskin.com
Shaklee 4747 Willow Road Pleasanton, CA 94588	800.SHAKLEE T 925.924.2000 F. 925.924.2862 www.shaklee.com or www.shaklee.net
Victoria Creager Collection 240 East 47 Street, suite 34-B New York, NY 10017	T 212.759.5476 F 212.751.3376
Weekenders, USA 3874 Riviera Drive San Diego, CA 92109	T 858.270.6737 F 858.274.7878 www.weekenders.com
Worth Collection, Ltd. 37 West 57 Street New York, NY 10022	212.944.9503 www.worthcollection.com

Cool Web Sites

www.all-biz.com	Online databases, business services Articles on business issues
www.amazon.com	Books and publications
www.bn.com	Barnes and Noble books and more
www.busines-plan.com	
www.claris.com/smallbiz	Advice about marketing online, customer relations and finance
www.geocities.com/WallStreet/2924/list1.htm	Articles on business planning, incorporation, start-up costs plus
www.google.com	Great search engine
www.ideacafe.com	
www.isquare.com	Advice for small biz professionals
www.ivillage.com	Women's center
www.morebusiness.com	Sample business agreements, time-saving templates, advice
www.lowe.org/smbiznet	Small/biz consultants, books, documents
www.newsletterinfo.com	Newsletter resources
www.nici.com/response	How to cut costs, improve response
www.oxygen.com	Women's center
www.smartbiz.com	How-to resources, news briefs
www.smartship.com	Shipping rates
www.women.com	

SAMPLE DOCUMENTS

Lynne Henderson Marks – Bio

Lynne Henderson Marks, President of London Image Institute has an unparalleled background in the arena of image and is among the most experienced in the world. After graduating in French and Psychology from London University she did pioneer Post Graduate research in Body Language and Nonverbal Communication skills, when it was virtually uncharted territory!

As a professor and head of one of the image and fashion departments at the London College of Fashion, she became experienced in image, design, tailoring, garment construction, fashion show production and modeling. She has worked for years in the areas of photographic and stage makeup, and has produced and directed hundreds of fashion-show extravaganzas.

As a corporate trainer, she provides programs in image management, communication skills, customer service, corporate protocol and presentation skills, to companies such as American Express, The Weather Channel, Coca-Cola, AT&T and CNN Sports.

With over twelve years experience in corporate identity and corporate culture design, she has designed and delivered courses in leadership, sales, customer service, management and executive team development, in companies such as United Airlines, Pacific Dunlop, Minnesota Mutual and Coca-Cola Enterprises. Lynne's individual clients are among some of the top U.S. executives and politicians to whom she coaches professional development, visual, nonverbal, interpersonal communication and presentation skills.

She is co-author of "The Perfect Fit: How to Start an Image Consulting Business".

She has been featured in Time magazine, Women's Day, Elle Magazine, CNN News and Glamour, and has been quoted on numerous occasions in the national and international media. She has served on the board of the Association of Image Consultants International, was president 1995-96 and received the AICI Award of Excellence for Education in 1998. She is Past President of IACET, The International Association for Continuing Education and Training.

In May 2002 Lynne was awarded the 2002 IMAGE MAKERS INDUSTRY AWARD OF EXCELLENCE (IMMIE) for her commitment to the Image Industry.

Dominique Isbecque - Bio

Dominique Isbecque, AICI, CIP, is Founder and President of DominiQue IsbecQue International, a professional development and image communications consulting firm based in Manhattan. She is considered the coach's coach.

During the last 20 years she has coached and trained thousands of individuals from executives and media personalities to support and sales staff, in the art of perception management, business etiquette and customer service. She has advised such corporations as Clairol, PricewaterhouseCoopers LLP, Robert Marston Public Relations, The American Bankers Association, Screen Actors Guild and AT&T on interpersonal image communications, personal promotion strategies and perception management. Dominique is a founder and Past President of the Association of Image Consultants International (AICI), Coordinator and Adjunct Instructor of the Certificate Program in Image Consulting at Fashion Institute of Technology. She is certified in color and image by Personal Spectrums, as a DiSC distributor and coach by Inscape, as a Certified Strategist by Coach U and in media training by Robert Marston Public Relations.

Dominique has been instrumental in building the field of image and personal communications through her speaking engagements, seminars, TV appearances and radio guest spots. She has written for and been featured in such national publications as The New York Times, Vogue, Glamour, Forbes and the Color Association of the United States' - Color Compendium Dictionary. Dominique was honored with the 1996 IMMIE Award for her personal and professional commitment to the Industry by AICI and with the 2001 Award of Excellence.

Dominique's firm belief in personal service drives her work as a consultant. She says, " Image directly impacts the way that we and the world perceive us. A clear outer identity that is aligned with our personal qualities and skills will positively effect our interactions with others. Self-confidence, personal effectiveness and our ability to deal with change are greatly empowered by the awareness and mastery of personal communication tools. Let us use them and make dreams happen."

Dominique has held positions as President of Beyond Fashion Inc. in New York, Director of Training for LOOK Consulting International and was the first national spokesperson for 1-800-FLOWERS. In addition, she is co-author of *The Perfect Fit, How to Start an Image Consulting Business*. Her background also includes work as a photographer and documentary filmmaker. Born in Africa and raised in both Belgium and the United States, Ms Isbecque now resides in New York City. She holds a B.A. in Contemporary Arts, is fluent in French and conversant in Spanish.

SAMPLE STRUCTURE FOR OUTLINING YOUR BIO

I.   Who are you?
Your name, title, company name, and location of your business

Marjorie Consultant, principle of MC Executive Imaging Group, of Bigtown, USA ...

II.   What do you do?
Description of products or services

Ms. Consultant provides personal consulting and training to individuals and corporate groups on image, personal presentation, and verbal and nonverbal communication. Her clients become equipped with tools and skills to successfully maneuver through their business and social situations.

III.   What qualifies you to be an expert?
Your background, experience and clients

In her 10 years as Account Executive of ABC Public Relations, Ms. Consultant worked in the media preparation of all spokespersons, helping her clients present clear visual and verbal messages on camera. In addition, she assisted in both the Welfare-to-Wages and Looking Good Cancer recovery programs to teach professional image, cosmetic application, interviewing skills, and other confidence-building skills.

IV.   What is your education, affiliations or awards?

Ms. Consultant graduated from VeryFine University with a B.A. degree in Communications and Public Relations and a minor in marketing. She is a member of the Association of Image Consultants International, the National Speakers Association, the Chamber of Commerce, and the local Community Planning Board, from which she received an award for work as the spearhead of the Beauty and Cancer Awareness campaign that raised funds to open a new hospital wing.

This is one method for writing a bio. The exact sequence may be shifted depending upon what you wish to emphasize and your business and consulting style.

SAMPLE LIST OF SERVICES TO INDIVIDUAL CLIENTS

Color Analysis
A 30-minute consultation within which we identify your optimum color palette for clothing, makeup, and hair color coordination. You will discover which colors to use to convey particular messages about you and which colors to avoid and why. You receive a personal color reference chart.

Image Assessment
A 60-minute session within which we identify the styles of clothing best suited to enhance your features and that will support your wardrobe and lifestyle needs. We will discuss fabrics, patterns, combinations, accessories, and hairstyle options. You will receive a workbook with personalized information for your reference.

Closet Analysis
A two- to three-hour session in your home to assess your current wardrobe. We begin with a discussion on your goals and will then select clothes that will help convey the visual messages to support you in attaining your goals. We will categorize your clothes into the *"wearables"*, *"questionables"*, and *"unbearables"* and come up with strategies to support you in filling any gaps. Examples include making a list of fill-in pieces, major items and/or accessories and including a workable budget. We will also take any *"unbearables"* to your favorite charity to make room for any new acquisitions.

Personal Shopping
A minimum of two hours is needed for a successful shopping session. After identifying your primary and secondary wardrobe needs and objectives, we will shop for these items together at designated vendor resources. Pre-shopping is included [*this is optional to the consultant*].

Etiquette, Protocol, Communication Styles and Special Event Coaching
These sessions are by the hour. After a preliminary assessment consultation we will determine the specific areas of focus that may include: dining, business manners, body language exercises, and media and job interview preparation. These sessions are designed to provide you with tools, skills practice, and increased confidence in those situations.

SAMPLE LETTER OF AGREEMENT WITH CORPORATE CLIENT

Marjorie Consultant
Principal
MC Executive Imaging Group
321 Maple Avenue, Suite 10
Big City, USA

June 1, 2001

Mr. John T. Jones
Human Resources Manager

123 Broad Street, 17 Floor
Big City, USA

Dear Mr. Jones,

As per our phone conversation and your request I hereby confirm that I will provide a Business Dress Casual Lunch N Learn presentation for Grow Your Finances Corporation. The program is currently scheduled to take place on [date]. One session will be conducted from 11:30 a.m. to 12:30 p.m., and the second session repeated from 12:30 to 1:30 p.m. There will be approximately 25–30 persons in each group. The agreed-upon package price is $1,400 with materials fee to be determined. I require a 50 percent nonrefundable deposit to reserve the date with the balance payable upon completion. If the program is cancelled within 14 days of the scheduled program date, the deposit can only be applied to a program rescheduled within 45 days.

I will present to Grow Your Finances Corporation staff members the company policy on Business Dress Casual according to the proposal. The content and format will be presented to your office in advance for review and approval.

I look forward to working with you and meeting with you again on [date].

Very Sincerely,

Marjorie Consultant,
Principal

Authors'note-
Please refer to Chapter Five and the Financial Ranges Matrix to guide you in costing your respective programs.

SAMPLE CONFIRMATION LETTER TO A CLIENT

Marjorie Consultant
Principal
MC Executive Imaging Group
321 Maple Avenue, Suite 10
Big City, USA

Dear Mr. Client,

Thank you for scheduling your Basic Color and Image Consultation with me. I want to confirm that your session is scheduled for Friday, (date and time). You will be coming to my studio location, which is at 123 West Main Street, Suite 5.

In your consultation I will

   1) evaluate your image and wardrobe objectives,
   2) select a suitable color palette, and
   3) assess an image development plan.

You may wear or bring an outfit you wish to have critiqued. The Basic Session will be about two hours long, and the fee is $___, payable by check or cash. If you would like to extend the session with an in-depth review and assessment of your current wardrobe, I will block out an additional hour and you could bring items from your wardrobe with you. The hourly rate for additional time is $___ per hour. I will leave the time open for you to decide next week.

I want you to get the most out of your consultation. To help you prepare, I'd like you to do a pre-assessment exercise. Enclosed is the questionnaire for you to fill out and fax back to me. Start reflecting upon your image and wardrobe goals, both immediate and/or long-term. We will discuss them in depth together. We will go over all of this together.

Should you have any questions please do not hesitate to call me. I will call you next week to confirm. I look forward to meeting you and to sharing in your image refinement process.

Very Sincerely,

Marjorie Consultant

SAMPLE INVOICE

Mrs. Harriet Client
123 Madison Street
Anytown, USA

Date

INVOICE

Personal Image Coaching
Sessions-
3 one-hour sessions
@ $XXX per hour $ XXX

_____

Total Amount Due $ XXX

Please make payable to :   Marjorie Consultant

And send to :   321 Maple Avenue, Suite 10
                                Big City, USA

Thank you for the opportunity to be of service!

PROGRAM INQUIRY CONTACT FORM

Entered in DataBase _____

Company _____	**Inquiry**
Address 1 _____	**Date** _____
Address 2 _____	**Ref'd By** _____
Contact _____	
_____ **Title** _____	**Phone** _____
Decision _____ **Title** _____	**Phone** _____
Maker	**Fax** _____
Special Info	**Email** _____

NATURE OF INQUIRY	AUDIENCE ANALYSIS
Presentation Training / Seminar Coaching	Size _____ // men ____ Women ____ Both ____Ages_____ Occupations- Regions from-
Objectives:	Context: Duration: **Requested Topics:** Prof. Image　　　　Communication Business Casual　　Customer Service Non Verbal　　　　Telephone Other:　　　　　　Networking 　　　　　　　　　Etiquette
Expectations:	Budget:　　　　　Booked for: Invoice Instructions:

Info Sent (what?): □ Corp. Pkt.   □ Letters   □ Additional (list):
Sent Via __(EM, Post, by hand)__ When _____ Rec'd _____
Follow up history:

Initial Meeting Set For:
Date-   Time-   Address-
With-

Bring: [ ]Corp Pkt.   [ ]Handouts   [ ]Other:
Purpose of meeting:

Observations:

Need:

Proposal Notes:

Follow-Up History:

CLIENT INQUIRY CONTACT FORM

Entered in DataBase _____

Company	_____	**Inquiry Date**	_____
Address 1	_____	**Ref'd By**	_____
Address 2	_____		
Contact	_____ **Title**_____	**Phone**	_____
Decision Maker	_____ **Title**_____	**Phone**	_____
		Fax	_____
Special Info		**Email**	_____

NATURE OF INQUIRY
Individual Services:
   ❑ Color Analysis
   ❑ Image Assessment
   ❑ Wardrobe
   ❑ Shopping
   ❑ Other
	Notes:

Objectives:	
Budget:	**Booked:**

Info Sent (what?)   ☐ Corp. Pkt.   ☐ Letters   ☐ Additional (list):

Sent Via ___(EM, Post, by hand)___   When _____   Rec'd _____

Follow up history:

MEDIA INQUIRY CONTACT FORM

Entered in DataBase _____

Company _____ Inquiry Date _____

Address 1 _____ Ref'd By _____

Address 2 _____

Contact _____ Title_____ Phone _____

Decision Maker _____ Title_____ Phone _____

Fax _____

Special Info Email _____

NATURE OF INQUIRY
- ❏ Print Story
- ❏ TV
- ❏ Radio
- ❏ Other

What's your Deadline?

Publishing/ Air Date?

Live or recorded?

What's the Angle or context?

Topics of Interest:

Prof. Image	Communication
Business Casual	Customer Service
Non Verbal	Telephone
Other:	Networking
	Etiquette

Can we get a copy?

Info Sent (what?): ☐ Corp. Pkt.   ☐ Letters   ☐ Additional (list):

Sent Via __(EM, Post, by hand)__   When _____   Rec'd _____

Follow up history:

To order additional copies of *The Perfect Fit,* Please complete the form below and mail with a check or credit card information.
Credit card orders may be faxed.

London Image Institute
4279 Roswell Road, # 102-318
Atlanta, GA 30342

Name		**ORDER BELOW**		
		Quantity	Unit cost	Total
Address			$34.95	
City		Sales Tax 7% GA residents		
State ZIP		Shipping Add $6.00 for single Book and $2, for each Additional copy		
Phone				
Email		Grand Total		
Shipping address (if different from above) Name		**METHOD OF PAYMENT**		
Address		☐ Check ☐ Money Order ☐ Visa ☐ Mastercard		
City		Make check or money order payable to: **London Image Institute**		
State ZIP				
Phone				
		Credit card number		
Email		Expiration date		
Signature				

To order additional copies of *The Perfect Fit,* Please complete the form below and mail with a check or credit card information. Credit card orders may be faxed.

London Image Institute
4279 Roswell Road, # 102-318
Atlanta, GA 30342

Name		**ORDER BELOW**		
		Quantity	Unit cost	Total
Address			$34.95	
City		Sales Tax 7% GA residents		
State ZIP		Shipping Add $6.00 for single Book and $2, for each Additional copy		
Phone				
Email		Grand Total		

Shipping address (if different from above)

Name

METHOD OF PAYMENT

Address

☐ Check   ☐ Money Order
☐ Visa   ☐ Mastercard

City

State ZIP

Make check or money order payable to:
London Image Institute

Phone

Email

Credit card number

Expiration date

Signature

Printed in the United States
21964LVS00001B/50

9 781589 392908